I0762744

TO
FROM
DATE

SHRUTHI PARKER
LIVING OPEN-HANDED
Devotions for Surrendering Control and Finding Joy in the Unexpected
DaySpring
LIVE YOUR FAITH

Living Open-Handed: Devotions for Surrendering Control and Finding Joy in the Unexpected

First Edition, October 2024

Published by:

21154 Highway 16 East
Siloam Springs, AR 72761
dayspring.com

Written by: Shruthi Parker
Cover Design by: Jessica Wei

Printed in China
Prime: U2693
ISBN: 979-8-88602-861-4

CONTENTS

INTRODUCTION

All right, I'm going to shoot it to you straight. I did not write this book from a place of being an expert but rather from a place of weakness. Repeatedly, challenging life circumstances kept me craving the balm of Scripture and truth every day, and the one little flame that kept my heart hopeful in the chaos was knowing God was good. I needed to hear it continually while also learning to surrender in all things, and this book was born. When I discovered my daughter was deaf, when my husband had cancer, when, when, when . . . God showed me I didn't need a situation to have a neat ending to have joy. I just needed Him. And oh, the joy there is! If out-of-control situations make you feel like you can't catch your breath, or fear feels too familiar day in and day out, this book is for you. I hope this devotional spurs you on toward the truth that you can find abundant peace and unbelievable joy even in the chaos. I hope any fear creeping into your heart is uprooted and, instead, substituted with bright, replenishing faith. God doesn't give us more than we can handle with Him. So give it to Him. Live open-handed, my friends.

Cheers,

HIS WINGS WON'T GET WEARY

But those who hope in the LORD
will renew their strength.
They will soar on wings like eagles;
they will run and not grow weary,
they will walk and not be faint."

ISAIAH 40:31

The first ten weeks of my third pregnancy were uneventful, and I couldn't believe how lucky we were. Then, I got the call that my baby had a 95 percent chance of being born with Down syndrome. I had no idea what to expect, and researching Down syndrome only brought me startling, outdated facts and stats. It took us some time to regain our footing, but we did so with the right wisdom, community, and peace from the Holy Spirit—until I went into spontaneous preterm labor at thirty weeks. I can still remember the smell of that pizza joint. Nothing could have prepared me for the next couple of months. The birth plan went out the door; I didn't see my daughter for the first fourteen hours; and I couldn't kiss her until eight weeks after her birth when I finally brought her home.

I will tell you that I don't know if I would have gotten through all of that without the Lord. Truly. Not of my own

strength, that is for sure. This picture Isaiah 40:31 gives us of having our strength renewed because we hope in the Lord was the epitome of that season. God held us up in His wings so we didn't have to struggle to fly. His strength kept me going. If you're in a season where circumstances feel out of control and you are exhausted, I have good news for you. You are not alone. He renews your strength so that you soar like an eagle instead of hobbling alone. Instead of breaking down from exhaustion, you will run and not grow weary with Him. You will walk and not be faint. Hope in the Lord does not put you to shame. Hope in Him today, tomorrow, and every day you need, because His love will never run out on those He calls His!

REFLECT

Where do you need the Lord to renew your strength? He can do all things. Ask Him. He's waiting for you.

Dear Lord, thank You for always being with me. You have renewed my strength more times than I can count, and I pray You help me remember that when life feels too much! You are so faithful. Amen.

JOY IN ASKING

"You haven't done this before.
Ask, using My name, and you will receive,
and you will have abundant joy."

JOHN 16:24 NLT

If you had three wishes, what would they be? Any movie or book you read shows that those wishes usually would end in chaos. Why? Because the giver of those wishes isn't invested in the wish maker's life or well-being. And then we have God. We know that God is not a genie. He's not just handing out three wishes left, right, and center. He's not confined to a lamp. He's ingrained in our lives, past, present, and future. He is eternal, and He is our good, good father. And what good father doesn't hear his child?

Sometimes, a father has to say no. Sometimes, a father has to say not yet. Sometimes, a father has to say, "I know you think this is best, but let me redirect you." But sometimes, a father says "YES, I'd love to do that for you!" We will never know if we don't ask. So, do you make your requests known to God or assume He will say no? God wants what is best for you and what is best for me. But His best and His timeline may look different than what we think is best and when we think it should happen.

Do you trust Him? Do you trust the One who knit you together? Trust then translates to His timing, plans, and nos and yeses. And when we ask as Scripture tells us, we will receive something—whether that's a no, not yet, not like that, or a yes—that our joy may be abundant!

REFLECT

Do you trust that you can ask God? Do you trust that however He answers is for your best and for your joy?

Dear Father in heaven, thank You for all the ways You care for me. Please help me remember that You are not far off, unaware of my circumstances. You are in the details of my life, and I am so grateful for that. I pray over those unanswered questions in my life today. Help me trust Your timing and Your decisions. Please give me peace and joy no matter the result.

JOY IN NEW MERCIES

The steadfast love of the Lord never ceases;
his mercies never come to an end;
they are new every morning;
great is your faithfulness.
LAMENTATIONS 3:22–23 ESV

"Mommy, I'm awake! I'm done sleeping! I want milk!" Good thing they're so cute. As soon as you wake up, what do you do every morning without fail? And no, I'm not talking about ideally, like running at 5:00 a.m. (If this is you–go you, seriously). I'm talking about habits that you do no matter what from muscle memory. I brush my teeth, put my contacts in, and head to the kitchen for coffee with my husband. No matter how complex the previous day was, those three stay consistent the following morning. What does Scripture tell us we can expect from God every morning? His steadfast love. His never-ending mercies. His great faithfulness.

Do you think about that? That is far more important and consistent than my routine will ever be. So much in life is out of our control. No matter the load you go to bed with, your mornings are a chance for all to be made new because the Word tells us this. We don't wake up from sleep refreshed just because of hours of unconsciousness. We

wake up refreshed because of the truth of this Scripture. Yes, we might have to tune our minds to this truth in the morning, but we can do that with repetition! We can create the habit of remembering His love, mercies, and faithfulness are complete and for us every morning. And when we remember these things, we wake up with a fresh capacity for the new day, no matter what comes our way.

Remember this the next time you go to bed, shaken or worn out by the unexpected day you've just had. We have God with us! Expect His love, mercy, and faithfulness to saturate your day from morning to morning. It's all we need!

REFLECT

Are you muscling through your day alone? Are any unexpected circumstances weighing you down today? Where can you release the pressure to do it alone and trust that God is with you?

Dear Lord, You see all that I have on my plate today. Please help me remember Your unending love, mercies, and faithfulness throughout my day, as my memory might forget. Keep me close to You and remind me that all of these are new every morning. Amen.

UNEXPECTED PROVISION

"Give us this day our daily bread."

MATTHEW 6:11 ESV

We are so used to buying items in bulk these days. One box of cereal? Why not buy three for the price of two? Or better yet, six for the price of three, and you will get free bagels too! That should surely last you all month and then some! We are in a culture of maximizing and taking more than we need for this day alone because it's convenient, makes companies more profitable, and reduces our reliance on the supply. Buying in bulk can be helpful, especially with several people in your home. But we cannot translate that way of life into our spiritual life. That is not how God works. He doesn't give us a bulk of love, patience, or faith one day to use for a month. Church is not a wholesale store where you can shop for the fruit of the Spirit. He offers us all we need in a day, every day. So what are you lacking today that you need to ask Him for? Or have you assumed that what you received some time ago is supposed to sustain you for days to come?

In Scripture we read, "Give us this day our daily bread." Have you asked for the Father's bread today? Bread in Scripture was the primary form of nourishment. Most of the wages people of the New Testament earned would go to supplying this necessary bread for their families. And Jesus tells us that He is the bread of life (John 6:35). He can give us our daily bread regardless of what is going on in our lives. Start with that simple prayer. When my daughter was in the NICU for fifty-three days, this was the main prayer I prayed every morning. "Please, Lord, even though it feels like chaos in these unexpected circumstances, give me joy, provide me perseverance, and supply me with sustenance. Please give me my daily bread." And you know what? He absolutely delivered.

REFLECT

Have you paused and asked God for what you need today?

Dear Lord, thank You so much for another day. Thank You for giving me all I need every day. Today, I ask for Your unending joy, a peace that surpasses all understanding, and Your nearness. Amen.

GOOGLE DOESN'T KNOW IT ALL

Trust in the Lord with all your heart
and lean not on your own understanding;
in all your ways submit to Him,
and He will make your paths straight.

PROVERBS 3:5–6

What was your last web search? Mine was about lymph nodes in our armpits. There's not much more to say there! I got the information I needed, but isn't it wild to live in an age where almost all information is available at our fingertips? We don't have to sit in the unknown for long at all. What's the weather? 84 degrees until 2:00 p.m. How far is that restaurant? 2.6 miles with no traffic. Is our flight delayed? By 37 minutes due to the north winds. The internet has enabled us to search for anything at any given time. And the answers are conveniently detailed.

But Google doesn't know a single detail about tomorrow and certainly doesn't know anything about eternity. Some things aren't instant and understood. No matter how much information you know, nothing takes the place of trusting God. Proverbs 3:5–6 encourages us to trust the Lord with all our heart and not rely on our own understanding in any situation. When was the last time you opened

your hands and said, "God, You got this. I trust that You got this"? For me, it was when I couldn't get through to make an appointment at the doctor's office. In moments like these, my instinct is to get angry at the pace of the medical system. And while I'm frustrated to have to be waiting this long for test results, it also reminds me that these are not answers I can Google search. This is not information that I can control or study. Instead, I have to keep my hands open and say, "God, I trust You with all my heart. I know You see all of this happening, and I know You care! I trust You in every appointment, phone call, and interaction. I'm leaning on You, knowing You're holding me up."

REFLECT

Where are you leaning on your own understanding? Are your hands gripped tightly, or have you opened them? Surrender it with me.

Say it with me. "God of goodness and grace, today I trust You with ______. I acknowledge You in all of this, and I lean on You. Thank You for caring for me and for making my paths straight. Amen."

COMPARISON IS A SIGN OF DISTRUST

"Consider how the wild flowers grow.
They do not labor or spin.
Yet I tell you, not even Solomon in all his splendor
was dressed like one of these."

LUKE 12:27–28

How old is your daughter again?" I asked. "Fourteen months!" she responded. Yup, just as I thought, her daughter was only a month older than my youngest, and yet my daughter was sitting in the stroller instead of playing. Why? Because she couldn't keep up with the other kids as they ran, jumped, and climbed. My daughter was born with Down syndrome, which physically includes lower muscle tone than the typical child. This means that her timeline to do what typical kids her age are doing takes longer. Almost immediately, my mood plummeted. We've all read the saying, "Comparison is the thief of joy," right? Oof, I can attest to that. I wish it were as easy as saying, "Well, just don't compare!" But sometimes, telling ourselves to stop comparing means we hinder breaking down why we compare in the first place, which is necessary to stop comparing.

Why *was* I comparing? Because I felt like she was left

out, I was impatient, and most of all, I didn't trust God's timeline and provision for her. But as Scripture tells us, the wildflowers don't toil and labor, and yet they grow exactly the way God intends. Why did I let comparison steal my joy and amplify my doubts about my beautiful wildflower? So what if it takes her a little longer to do the things that kids her age are doing? So what if she never does something they do? She has her deliberate timeline, and my role as her mom isn't to rush or push her but to guide and support her. I don't need to toil and labor and worry! I need to trust.

The next time I saw this mom friend, I combated any initial comparative thoughts with one of openhanded trust. Over time, that surrender has meant greater joy in playdates and trust in God's plan for my daughter.

REFLECT

Where are you when it comes to comparing in your life? Do you see how it steals your joy? Where is your distrust louder than your trust?

Dear Lord, I say that I trust You, but I keep parts of me hidden. Help me open my hands and release my grip. I don't want comparison or worry to take any more time. Amen.

PRAY AND PRAISE, ALWAYS

Is anyone among you in trouble?
Let them pray. Is anyone happy?
Let them sing songs of praise.

JAMES 5:13

A while ago, my husband and I disagreed about the importance of date night. When he said, "I feel like I'm the only one prioritizing time together," I was ready with several retorts ranging from "It's been hard to find childcare" to "I just am so tired by 5:00 p.m. . . ." We didn't leave that interaction with a solution, and I had to leave for a playdate. I was driving the kids to a playdate soon after, and the music in the car wasn't working, so I had no choice but to sit with my irritated thoughts when the first half of James 5:13 came into my head. *I guess I could pray about it*, I thought halfheartedly. But that's one thing I love about prayer. You can be so far from where you want to be when you start, but once you commune with God and ask to be in His will, He helps you move into a place of trust that He will give you precisely what you need. You don't need a solution to have God's peace. So, I talked to Jesus and said, "I truly

want to spend time with my husband, but I'm also tired and don't know where else to look for childcare. Can You please help me out?"

At the park, I told a mom friend about this recent discussion when another woman sitting near us said, "I'd be happy to do childcare on your date nights!" I had seen her several times because the kiddos she watched were friends with my littles. My friend smiled at me and said, "Well, look at God hearing you and answering your prayer." On the drive home, I didn't even need my music playing. I went to the second half of James 5:13, which says, "Is anyone happy? Let them sing songs of praise." And sing songs of praise I did!

REFLECT

Is prayer the first thing you go to in times of trouble and joy? What is your prayer life like?

Father God, You know everything tossing about in my heart even better than I do. Please help me remember to pray in the peaks and the valleys because I want to trust You with it all! Amen.

YOU CANNOT WIN GOD'S APPROVAL

Go, eat your food with gladness,
and drink your wine with a joyful heart,
for God has already approved what you do.

ECCLESIASTES 9:7

People try to "win points" with God through good deeds, donating, giving up vices, and more, but ultimately, it's the heart behind why you do those things. Are you seeing them as a transaction with God, hoping to receive His favor and approval? Or is the motivation due to the overflow from your heart, from already knowing you're approved of? It's easy to get lost in the toil. Early on in my career, I was determined to write about my faith every Sunday, even when all I really wanted to do was rest. I told myself that if I didn't do it, then God wouldn't approve of my work and, in turn, He wouldn't approve of me. But did God ever tell me that? No. I put that strange, self-righteous pressure on myself. I wish I could go back in time and tell myself that rest is pleasing in God's eyes, but I don't know if my younger self would have believed it.

Do you find yourself toiling for God's approval? Oh, friend, in Christ, we are free. We are approved of. We are chosen. We strive to live like Christ not because we want

God to love us but because He already does. And not only has He already approved of us, but He also wants good things for us. He wants us to enjoy the life we have been given. So many "religious" people believe that living in a way that diminishes joy and light shows how serious they are about their faith. In Ecclesiastes, we see God say, "GO!" He tells us that whatever we do, we should do it with gladness and joy! Do you live in a way that displays how God has already approved of you? Are you living in freedom while also pursuing righteousness?

REFLECT

Where in your life do you find yourself trying to gain God's approval? Do you find having a joyful, glad spirit in your everyday actions easy or challenging?

Dear Lord, please help me remember that
work is a good thing but not the main thing,
that it is not a way for me to earn Your approval.
You come first in all things. Amen.

CHRIST > CIRCUMSTANCES

You became imitators of us and of the Lord,
for you welcomed the message in the midst
of severe suffering with the joy given by the Holy Spirit.

I THESSALONIANS 1:6

Joy isn't dependent on our circumstances. We know that because our joy comes from Jesus. But do we live that way?

- If the laundry isn't done, can we still have joy?
- If the work promotion doesn't come, can we still have joy?
- If the relationship doesn't last, can we still have joy?
- If the number on the scale changes, can we still have joy?
- If we don't get invited, can we still have joy?

We can. We absolutely can. In the most brutal of circumstances, the believers in Thessalonica were reminded of the complete and lasting joy in Jesus (see today's Scripture). People think Christians have an easy life. Even I thought my life after knowing Jesus would be easy, because I assumed *blessed* meant *ease*. Oh, the naivety. Has life been blessed?

Beyond belief! But uncomplicated? Complexity and I are good friends at this point!

But seriously, I haven't met a single believer who would describe their life as difficulty free, yet their joy empowered by the divine presence of God within us (otherwise known as the Holy Spirit) is unmatched. In a world that wants you to believe your joy depends on what you have, what you make, who you know, and what you achieve, say no thank you. My joy isn't dependent on my circumstances! Say it and believe it. On Christ, the solid rock we stand.

REFLECT

What circumstances in your life are determining your joy? Is it your family? Work? Body image? Relationships? The news? How do you reflect God's goodness and nature, even in the most challenging seasons?

Come, Holy Spirit. Fill me up with the joy only You can. Everything else, however good, is fleeting. Only Your joy lasts forever, and I ask this today, knowing You can do this. Amen.

GOOD MEDICINE

A joyful heart is good medicine,
but a crushed spirit dries up the bones.

PROVERBS 17:22 ESV

What is your most used medicine? After three surgeries in our family in the last three months, I'd have to say ibuprofen. It cuts through pain, and, hello, it's bubble gum flavored. Scripture tells us about another type of medicine: a joyful heart. There is such power in joy, and we can always access joy through the power of the Holy Spirit. When life gets tough, does that mean we cannot feel sad? Not at all! But we can hold both our situational sadness and choose a joyful heart because God is always good no matter the circumstances. And access to joy through Him is always present. People spend too much of their lives thinking of the worst-case scenario, wallowing in worries, and creating more stress in their souls. Then they wonder why they feel drained, hopeless, and crushed. I'm not talking about diagnosed mental health conditions here, because that's not a choice. However, most people have the choice to create a thought process that leads to a joyful heart or a crushed spirit.

God doesn't want us to live with a crushed spirit. He wants us to focus on what is good (Philippians 4:8). He

wants us to enjoy Him (Psalm 73:25). He wants to walk with us when the burden feels overwhelming (Psalm 55:22). This is also why community matters. We were made to be with people! We don't have to remove ourselves, give ourselves medicine, and then return to society. If a joyful heart is good medicine, bring that around your friend with the crushed spirit and let them do that for you too. I learned this deeply in motherhood. It has been such "good medicine" for me in the beautiful trenches of toddlerhood. And a joyful heart helps out any heart in the trenches! You don't need a prescription for this medicine. It is freely offered to you today. Ask for it.

REFLECT

Does joy always look like happiness? No. But joy can be as simple as prompting your heart to be thankful for God's blessings even in challenging circumstances. Remember God's faithfulness in your life today.

Dear Lord, please fill my heart with Your joy. Please help me give that good medicine to a friend, neighbor, or stranger I encounter today.

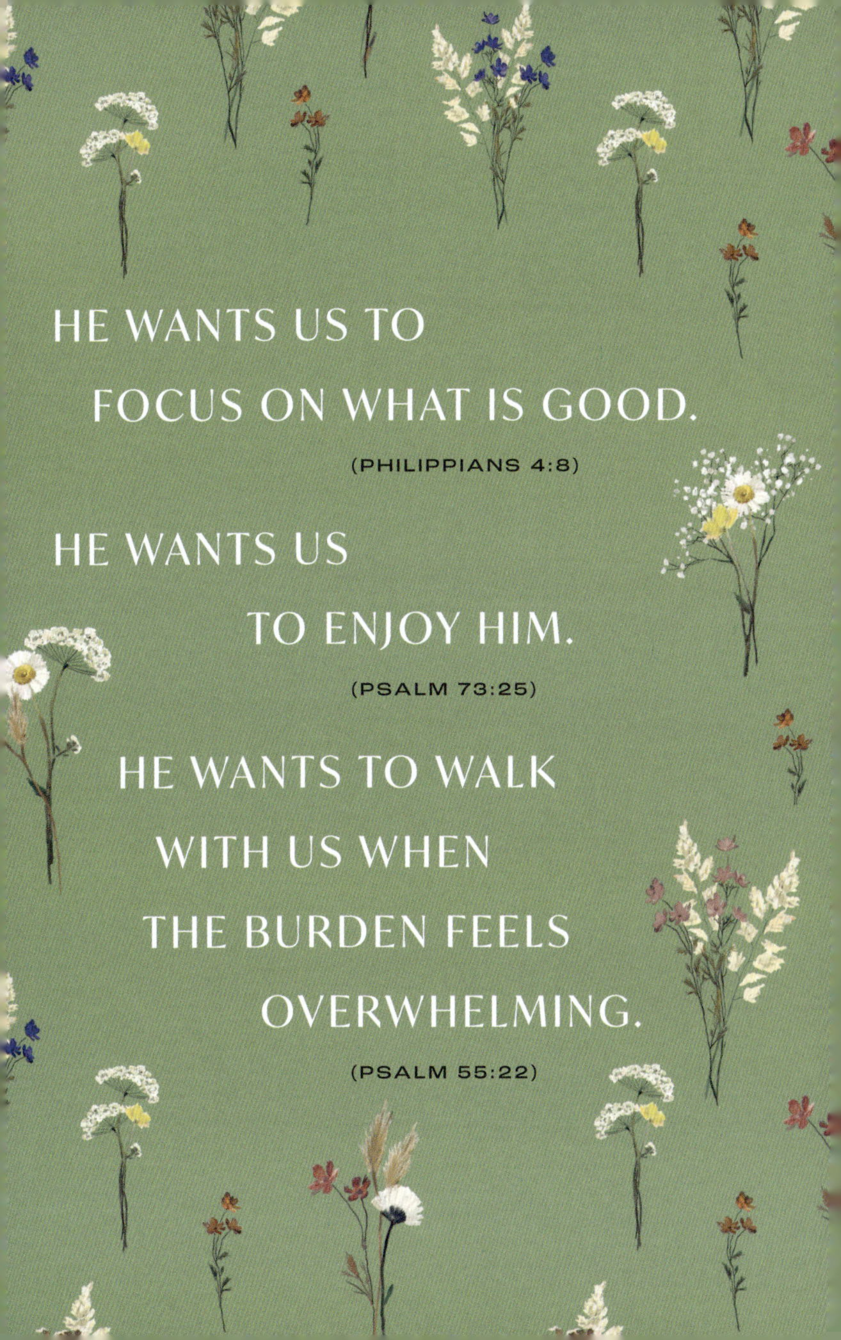
HE WANTS US TO
FOCUS ON WHAT IS GOOD.
(PHILIPPIANS 4:8)
HE WANTS US
TO ENJOY HIM.
(PSALM 73:25)
HE WANTS TO WALK
WITH US WHEN
THE BURDEN FEELS
OVERWHELMING.
(PSALM 55:22)

THANK YOU FOR MY TRIALS

Consider it pure joy, my brothers and sisters, whenever you face trials of many kinds, because you know that the testing of your faith produces perseverance. Let perseverance finish its work so that you may be mature and complete, not lacking anything.

JAMES 1:2–4

When trials come my way but I remember today's Scripture (James 1:2–4), I handle them entirely differently than my instinct wants me to. My instinct wants me to throw a massive pity party and spend too many minutes wondering why this is happening. Can you relate? But when my mind is trained by Scripture and remembers the truth of James 1, I rejoice because I know if I keep my eyes on Jesus, it makes me more like Him! Honestly, lucky me! I understand, okay, this is necessary for me to be mature and complete, not lacking anything. And that simple mindset shift makes all the difference in how I walk through a trial.

Yes, even my daughter's deaf diagnosis, my husband's cancer diagnosis, my son's last-minute surgery, my ear closing up for two days and being unable to hear . . . all of it has a purpose. Thank God our trials have a purpose, even

if we don't want them. Think about Jesus in the garden. He didn't want to go on the cross, but He did want to do God's will. He asked God to take the cup from Him if it was God's will—more than once. But God didn't take that cup away from Him. And so, as Hebrews 12:2 reminds us, "For the joy set before Him He endured the cross, scorning its shame, and sat down at the right hand of the throne of God." The way Jesus navigates trials is our best example. He talks to God about what He wants, submits to God's will (as that is where the greatest joy is), and perseveres till the very end. How great is our God, and what an example to consider it all joy!

REFLECT

What trials are you facing today? Do you believe that there is purpose here?

Dear Lord, please help me persevere in my trials when I grow weary. I know this is all for my maturing and completion, and I find great comfort in that. I want to consider it all joy. Amen.

COVERED IN HIS WINGS

He will cover you with His feathers.
He will shelter you with His wings.
His faithful promises are
your armor and protection.

PSALM 91:4 NLT

To the one who feels like life is a series of constant fights, I hope you know you can leave your battles, big and small, in God's capable and steady hands. The Lord never stops working in your favor. I hope you feel confident to tell those anxious scenarios you create in your mind that God has the last word. God never bows down to the world. You don't have to be your own defense. Trust your Shield, your Refuge! Like Psalm 91:4 reminds us, "He will cover you with His feathers. He will shelter you with His wings. His faithful promises are your armor and protection." What a stunning picture. Imagine yourself wrapped in God's wings, His mighty feathers shielding you from the evil trying to make its way to you. As someone prone to overthinking, this verse is a balm to my racing mind. Nothing is really in my control, and that frees me so much! When you and I rely

on God to fight our battles, we take a healthy step away from joy-sucking thought patterns like anxiety, fear, and hopelessness. Joy is ours when we abide in Jesus. So let's allow His Word to fill our minds, pray regularly, and trust that His faithful promises are our armor and protection!

REFLECT

Where do you need to believe God has you covered with His wings today? Is it a relationship, work situation, or something else? Can you release that to Him today and trust that He is thoroughly invested in the situation and already fighting for you?

O God of the heavens, thank You so much for Your feathers, which shield me from so much I am unaware of. God, I come before You thinking about this situation today. I know You have protected me and will continue to protect me. I pray You help me surrender this to You and trust You with it. You are a mighty, powerful, and protective God, and I want to trust You today. In Your name, I pray. Amen.

BOAST IN YOUR WEAKNESS

"My grace is sufficient for you,
for My power is made perfect in weakness."
Therefore I will boast all the more gladly
about my weakness,
so that Christ's power may rest on me.

II CORINTHIANS 12:9

During my last two pregnancies, which were especially difficult, I had a few strangers message me saying, "Make things right with God. This difficulty is happening because you've done something wrong." How sad for them to believe trials meant God's judgment, and how hopeless they must feel when life does get tough.

Some believe that a trial falls on people because of God's anger. Those who say that if you know the Lord, your life will be filled with wins, comforts, and riches believe a deadly lie. The Christian life was never defined as an easy life. Look at Christ. He lived the most holy life of all, and that included enduring the cross! Look at the lives of all His disciples. If we are following Christ, we need to look at our own lives. Not only do we have trials in our lives, but we are also weak, and that's uncomfortable, especially in a culture that brags about self-sufficiency. One of the best parts about knowing we are not enough is that we notice and appreciate God's mighty power most in this weak state.

When you face trials, trust that God hears you and that the way He answers is best. Rather than resent His not answering your prayers the way you wanted, try boasting in your weaknesses, and see if it gives you the grace and strength through the Holy Spirit to not only endure but to endure with joy.

REFLECT

Where are you weak today? Can you allow Christ to be strong in places you are weak so that His power may rest on you?

God, I am so grateful that I am not enough. I am so thankful I don't have to fake it till I make it. I am glad that in my weak state, Your power is made perfect. Help me boast all the more gladly about my weakness today so that Christ's power may rest on me! Amen.

SURRENDER CAN STILL MEAN MOVE

Then his sister said to Pharaoh's daughter,
"Shall I go and call you a nurse
from the Hebrew women
to nurse the child for you?"

EXODUS 2:7 ESV

When we think about living open-handed, there's a fine line and a healthy difference between surrendering everything and doing nothing. Sometimes God opens the door, and sometimes He wants us to open the door while still trusting Him. Think about dating. It would be strange to trust God with dating while sitting at home all day without social interaction, right? Or think about the next job you're going to apply for. While you trust God with your future, you'd still update your résumé and apply, wouldn't you? There's an appropriate level of involvement that comes with living open-handed. Your hands aren't in control, but you make moves that align with Scripture and the wisdom God can give you. He can redirect or shut those moves down, but you still move.

Take Moses's sister, Miriam, for example. If you remember, Moses was born when Pharaoh ordered all baby boys to be thrown into the Nile River. While his mother kept him

hidden for three months, Miriam kept a watch out for him as a baby. She helplessly kept a watch out for him even on the day when his mother left him in a basket on the Nile. What could she possibly do as he floated away from her down the river? When she saw that Pharaoh's daughter was interested in him, she courageously suggested getting a Hebrew woman to nurse him for the princess. She surrendered her brother's life while also taking action for her goal, which was to care for her brother. In that quick thinking, she also blessed her mother, as her mother was the Hebrew nurse the princess hired.

Surrendering your life to the Lord doesn't mean inaction. Move to the melody of the Holy Spirit. Tune in to what the Lord has in store for you, and keep your hands open in the process.

REFLECT

Where are you letting surrendering turn into stale inaction? Do you trust the hands that are moving?

Lord, You are the great orchestrator of my life. Help me see where I am not taking steps in faith even while I've surrendered. I want to do what You have for me. Please help me see it! Amen.

THE BEST ARMOR

You prepare a table before me
in the presence of my enemies.
You anoint my head with oil;
my cup overflows.

PSALM 23:5

When life feels overwhelming, I start to make lists of what I can control and what I cannot. Do you ever do that? It sounds silly, but I'll tell you that my "not in control" list is (a) always lengthier than I'd like and (b) a fabulous reminder to bring it all back to God. Not only is God the most qualified General to lead in battle, but He is also the most generous and prepared, as today's Scripture, Psalm 23:5, reminds us. When life is out of control or our enemies are all around us, we can wholly trust God to protect and guide us. When we depend on Him, we don't just get through the day, we stride confidently.

Imagine entering a banquet feast and having your enemies seated all around you but knowing you were completely safe and cared for. Those gawking at you wouldn't be able to touch a hair on your head because the God of the heavens was in your corner. That is how David, who wrote Psalm 23:5, feels in God's presence and how we can too! What is the significance of David saying God anoints him with oil? It

symbolizes God's blessing, protection, and favor. In ancient times, anointing with oil was a common practice used to honor guests or to set them apart for a higher purpose. David is saying that even in the midst of adversity, God sets him apart, calling him to a special purpose, calling him worthy. David says that his cup overflows; he has more than enough for his needs! This is how God cares for you, watches over you, and blesses you! Are you open to receiving that today?

REFLECT

Where do you need to trust that God has a table prepared for you in the presence of your enemies? Do you believe God not only protects you but also blesses you?

Dear Lord, thank You for the ways You guide me and protect me. Please help me remember that I am secure in You, that You bless me, and that I have more than I need in You. Amen.

THE GOD OF PEACE

Finally, brothers, whatever is true,
whatever is honorable, whatever is just,
whatever is pure, whatever is lovely,
whatever is commendable, if there is any excellence,
if there is anything worthy of praise,
think about these things.
What you have learned and received and heard
and seen in me—practice these things,
and the God of peace will be with you.

PHILIPPIANS 4:8–9 ESV

Let's make a list! Describe the various thoughts you entertained in your mind today. What does that list look like? My list for yesterday looks something like: worst-case scenario, irritated, helpless, prayerful, neutral, calm, peaceful. Clearly, there is a story of surrender there. It helped me end my day peacefully, even though I didn't start that way. Does the Bible have a list of what we should think about? Actually, it does! Philippians 4:8 reminds us to think of what is true, honorable, just, pure, lovely, commendable, excellent, and worthy of praise. God wants us to dwell, reflect, and ponder on that which illustrates His character. Why? Well, for one, what we think about has a compelling impact on our day. And two, even though there are so many popular practices about mindfulness and positive thinking,

those practices are incomplete without the One who made us, especially for true peace (Philippians 4:8).

When I received my daughter's diagnosis when she arrived ten weeks early and when she went to the NICU, I wouldn't have had the strength to go through my days if I kept dwelling on what was hard, painful, annoying, scary, worrisome, and anxious. Even if I started from a place of one of those, I learned to put into practice Philippians 4:8 so that the God of peace would be with me! He undoubtedly guarded my heart and mind against the mess and stress of my circumstances and blessed me with a peace that surpassed any understanding, even while we were very much still in the storm. He offers that freely to you today too. Receive it! Nothing compares to God's peace.

REFLECT

Consider what is true, honorable, just, pure, lovely, commendable, excellent, and worthy of praise. Let it soak in.

Dear Lord, so many things are competing in my mind daily for the greatest space on stage. Help me think about what is excellent or praiseworthy! O God of peace, be with me in every circumstance! Amen.

UNEXPECTED CONTENTMENT

I know what it is to be in need,
and I know what it is to have plenty.
I have learned the secret of being content
in any and every situation, whether well fed
or hungry, whether living in plenty or in want.
I can do all this through Him who gives me strength.

PHILIPPIANS 4:12–13

What does it mean to be content? Is it happy? Does it mean you have everything you need? Paul, who wrote today's Scripture, says even when he is hungry, he is content, so no, his needs were not always being met. Does it mean you have control? When Paul wrote this he was sitting in prison, so no, he more than likely had little control. How can Paul say he has learned the secret to being content? He says the secret to being content is through pursuing God's purposes for your life. God will give you everything you need to do the things He wants for you. God is not a fairy godparent granting wishes. We can ask Him for what we want, but what we want should align with what He wants for us first. Do you want what God has planned for you? Or is God part of the puzzle of your life, fitting in where you decide? When you want God's purposes for your life more than your schemes and dreams, you'll find peace and contentment that can endure every situation, as Paul describes! When he says he can do all this through Him who gives him strength, he's talking about doing God's plan for his life, not his own! That Scripture is often misused when people chase after their plans and then say, "Look, I can do anything I set my mind to because God gives me strength." No. That's not it! Sure, you can chase after all those things, and you may even have some success stories and accomplishments to share, but if you find that you are never genuinely content, it's because that's not what God has in store for you. What He has planned for you is made just for you, with the best for you in mind, and results in His glory.

REFLECT

What plans do you need to surrender at God's feet and say, "Not my will but Yours?"

God of all creation, You know me better than I will ever know myself. Help me let go of what I think I need or strive for, which will only make me empty and unfulfilled. Help me align my plans with Yours so I may know true contentment! Amen.

THE ONLY PERFECT ONE

God's way is perfect.
All the LORD's promises prove true.
He is a shield for all
who look to Him for protection.

PSALM 18:30 NLT

Think about all the people you trust. Say their names out loud. Have any of them ever made a mistake in their lives? You're probably thinking, well, they've all made mistakes. Do you still trust them? Think about yourself. Have you ever done something imperfectly? Does that prevent you from being trustworthy? You likely still trust that list of people since you listed them, and you hope to be seen as trustworthy since that's a quality in a good friend. Now, think about Psalm 18:30, which says that God's way is perfect and all His promises prove true. He has never broken a promise to us. He doesn't have a single imperfect way. And yet, can we confidently say that we trust Him always in all things with all things?

When my daughter was born ten weeks early, not a single medical professional could tell me why. They ran numerous tests, labs, and cultures and still didn't understand the situation. I had to consciously pick up my dependence, remove it from my doctor's bucket, and put it in the Lord's. I know His promises prove true and He promises never to forsake me (Deuteronomy 31:8), keep me in perfect peace (Isaiah 26:3), and strengthen me (Isaiah 41:10). Who would I rather trust? The medical professionals who couldn't understand what was happening or the One who created me and my daughter and whose way is always perfect and who is a shield for all who look to Him for protection? The answer was simple. What situation do you need to trust God with more than other resources?

REFLECT

Open your hands and trust the One whose way is perfect and whose promises are true. Cast your anxieties on Him and look to Him for protection. He is your steadfast shield.

Dear Lord of everything, thank You so much for the ways you care for every hair on my head. I bring this situation before You and ask that Your Holy Spirit give me the peace, patience, and self-control to hand it over to You. I don't want to put my trust in imperfect and untrue places. This is best with You. Help me believe that today. Amen.

THE NIGHT-LIGHT

So do not fear, for I am with you;
do not be dismayed, for I am your God.
I will strengthen you and help you;
I will uphold you with My righteous right hand.

ISAIAH 41:10

Every night, my kids ask me and my husband for several kisses, a few songs, a couple of stories, and a prayer. And if we don't turn on the night-light before we leave, chaos breaks loose. It doesn't matter how often I've told them not to be scared, they still insist that the black wolf bears will come out of the closet if I don't turn on the night-light for them. It sounds somewhat cute, but believe me, it can get tiring. Aren't I like that with God, though? Fearful, hesitant, scared even though He has said repeatedly that I should not fear. He has said it so many times that it's written in the Bible over one hundred times! And yet, I still worry. I still think of worst-case scenarios. I still act like things would be better if I had more control over my life. What a lack of faith! I may need a bright pink night-light too!

When God tells us not to fear, that He is with us, will strengthen us, and uphold us with His righteous right hand, how can that not be enough for me? Fear is an indicator that

faith needs a boost. And dismayed can mean distressed or anxious, usually at something unexpected. Where are you fearful? Dismayed?

Lord Jesus, You are so powerful and mighty. You are my ever-present refuge. Why do I succumb to fear in these places, Lord? I know Your promises are true and perfect. I know You will never leave me or forsake me. Help my unbelief! I do not want to sit in fear but rather trust You in all ways because Your ways are perfect. Help me translate that from my head to my heart, Lord! Amen.

REFLECT

We say our hope is in the Lord. But sometimes, security, success, knowledge of the future, and stability creep up in front of trusting the Lord. When it comes in front of God, it's an idol. What false gods do you find yourself putting some hope in? This could be a range of idols, from relationships to careers to self-help. Take some time to think through this.

GODLY SECURITY IN HUMAN INSTABILITY

Trust in the Lord with all your heart
and lean not on your own understanding;
in all your ways submit to Him,
and He will make your paths straight.

PROVERBS 3:5–6

How do you handle unanswered questions? Questions like should you stay in the same area you grew up and live close to family, or should you move somewhere new? Should you stay at your current job, or should you look for something new? Or questions like is now the time to start a family, or should you wait a few more years to get fully acclimated to being married? Being in a state of transition without clear steps forward is uncomfortable, isn't it? Sometimes do you just wish God would make you a neon sign in the sky that says, "Live here, work here, do this with your family"? But then you wouldn't have to have faith. Most of the unknowns in our lives are temporary. If we would just hang on a second, God would show us what the next steps would look like, yet instead of patiently waiting we tend to start searching for outcomes for ourselves. And why do we do this? Control. It's so tempting to take matters into our

own hands when we don't have the answers as soon as we would like. But what if we decided to pause and check in with our all-knowing God and remember these truths:

1. God's timing is perfect (Proverbs 16:9).
2. God's ways are excellent (Psalm 18:30).
3. God loves me (John 3:16).

If we truly believed these statements to be true, then we would know that the best way to handle unanswered questions is to release control, surrender ourselves before God, trust His perfect plan, and simply wait for His plan to unfold.

REFLECT

Where must you submit to Him and not lean on your understanding today?

God, You are not surprised by my life! You know full well what tomorrow holds for me, and You will make my paths straight if I lean on You and submit to You! Please help me do this today, empowered by Your Holy Spirit. I can trust You in all things because You are perfect. Amen.

REMEMBER
THESE TRUTHS:
GOD'S TIMING
IS PERFECT.
(PROVERBS 16:9)
GOD'S WAYS
ARE EXCELLENT.
(PSALM 18:30)
GOD LOVES ME
(JOHN 3:16)

THE ICE CREAM CONE

"Therefore you now have sorrow;
but I will see you again and your heart will rejoice,
and your joy no one will take from you."

JOHN 16:22 NKJV

There are so many ways we can take delight in the people, places, and things that surround us. We experience joy in close friendships; however, these relationships can also be taken away due to distance or misunderstandings. We finally splurged for that outfit we wanted; however, eventually it will fade or shrink or be ruined by a stain. We can pause and delight in the sunset that is filled with pink, purple, blue, and yellow; however, these moments are temporary, and once nighttime falls, the moment is over.

One day, I made the brilliant decision to go to the zoo in the middle of the hot Texas summer. Within five minutes, my entire family was sweating puddles. But when we found an ice cream stand, our lives were instantly brightened. Until we ate the ice cream and found ourselves in the hot sun again. So, what am I saying here? Jesus is our eternal ice cream cone? That's just silly, but also, sort of.

In John, Jesus tells His disciples that they will not see Him anymore and they will be persecuted. They are understandably distraught. But then He comforts them with

the truth that He will rise from the dead, go to the Father, and pour out His Spirit on them. Not only will they see Him again, but their joy will never be taken away. The same is true for us. Can you fathom that? There will come a day that our joy will never leave us. Fear will never make a home in us. We will never long for quick hits of fleeting pleasures on earth. Let's keep this perspective front of mind today and try to refocus our minds daily to rest in the true joy, security, and peace of a relationship with Christ. Because the truth is God is bigger than any earthly letdowns including misunderstandings, stains, nightfall, and even the summer heat in Texas.

REFLECT

What is your most recent version of my ice cream cone story? Do you believe you can find the greatest and most consistent joy today in a relationship with Jesus? Or is He an accessory while other things and people take turns filling your cup instead?

Dear Lord Jesus, I long for the day when my joy will not be taken away by my human limitations. Thank You for the joy-filled future You've secured for me. Amen.

JOY ALWAYS

You have put more joy in my heart
than they have when their grain and wine abound.

PSALM 4:7 ESV

True or false? Your circumstances do not dictate whether you can have joy. True. We all know that, but how many of us live in step with the truth that spiritual joy endures? I'll speak for myself. When push comes to shove, I have to be reminded that no matter the storm around me, I can have ultimate joy because of Jesus. If everything has to be squared away to encounter the perfect joy of God, is that really joy? Or is that my illusion of control? Let me tell you something. Control loves to masquerade as things other than what it is.

You can have real joy even in a messy house, moms. You can have perfect joy even when that end-of-year bonus doesn't come through. You can have true joy even when you get the diagnosis. Your joy doesn't have to hide even when your baby comes ten weeks early. You can have perfect joy even after another rejection. You can have true joy even when you are unsure how the funds will add up. You can have true joy even when you feel misunderstood. You can trust that God's joy is for you in every circumstance! These are all moments from my life that I had to exercise in faith the true joy offered to me through faith in Jesus. And you know what? I encountered that true joy in all of them. I may not have started there, but through surrender of my circumstances, I always ended there. In a time when grain was necessary for every meal and wine was essential for every event, Scripture says, they have more joy in their hearts than when they receive what they need daily and more. And the good news is, He is right here, ready to fill your cup with heavenly joy. Are your hands open and willing to receive it?

REFLECT

What circumstance or emotion prevents you from experiencing the joy God has for you today? If there is no hindrance, ask the Holy Spirit to come and fill you up with His joy.

Dear Lord, thank You for the innate joy You give us. It is beyond any outward happiness that could come from the "abundant harvests" of our lives. Please help me remember that! Amen.

CONFESSION IS BETTER THAN GLITTER

Have mercy on me, O God,
according to Your unfailing love;
according to Your great compassion
blot out my transgressions.

PSALM 51:1

Have you ever allowed glitter, slime, paint, or tie-dye in your house? It can make such a mess, ending up ruining your carpet, sticking in your hair, and staining tabletops. Needless to say, while the craft project may be fun at the time, the clean-up is not as enjoyable. And what makes it worse? When the ones who contributed to the mess refuse to own up to it, and you are left to find a way to wipe up the glitter and scrub up the slime. But here is a question to consider: are we too righteous or too embarrassed or too scared to admit the mess we've made when it comes to confessing our sins to God? Are we leaving God to wipe it all up without acknowledging that we left things in disarray?

There is so much freedom in confession, as David shows us in today's Scripture. We can always be honest with the Lord. Not only should we be, but we should also want to because He offers us a cleansing that nobody and nothing else can. Confession is one of the most significant forms of surrendering because you release your past to Him and trust

Him with the parts of your heart you want to keep hidden. David was a man after God's own heart, but He had a lot to confess! From adultery to murder, David knew the only one who could forgive him, wash him white as snow, and sanctify him was the Lord, so he threw himself at Jesus's compassionate feet in prayer, asking for mercy. David is a perfect example of humble and thorough confession and the freedom that comes from it.

Surrendering does not just mean your plans for your future. It can also mean your past. We all fall short, and where the Lord is, grace abounds. Meet Him there.

REFLECT

Confession is one of the sincerest forms of giving up control. What do you need to confess today? Without filter or fluff, be honest with the Lord like David.

Create in me a clean heart, O Lord of heaven! Only You can do this mighty and massive work. In a world of temptations, please renew my steadfast spirit and forgive the transgressions I've already committed. I come before You today, confessing these things with a humble and contrite heart. Help me be more like Jesus, Lord. Amen.

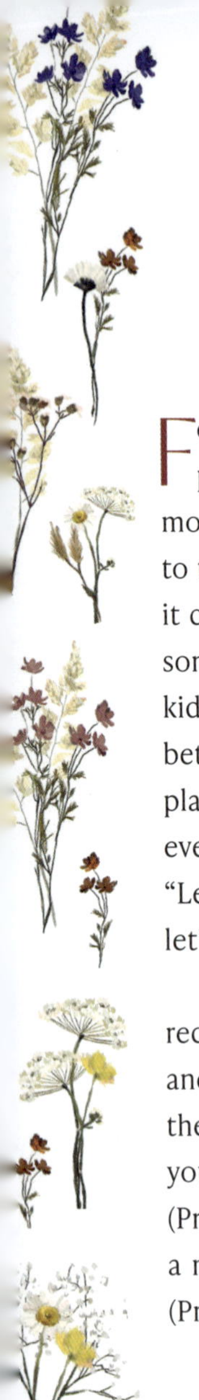

SHOULD I PLAN?

The heart of man plans his way,
but the LORD establishes his steps.

PROVERBS 16:9 ESV

For Christmas this year, three different people gifted me planners. I can't tell whether this means I need to plan more or that they all think I love planning. I've decided to take on the right mindset and assume the latter! When it comes to plans, my husband and I are in the middle of some big ones. We know this is for the betterment of our kids' futures, but sometimes I wonder where the line is between planning without fully trusting God and how to plan faithfully. Maybe you've struggled with this too, and even contemplated making another musical rendition of "Let Go, Let God." Before you head to the recording studio, let's see what Scripture says about planning.

The Bible tells us that "If you plan to do good, you will receive unfailing love and faithfulness" (Proverbs 14:22 NLT) and "Without counsel plans fail, but with many advisers they succeed" (Proverbs 15:22 ESV). It also says, "Commit your work to the LORD, and your plans will be established" (Proverbs 16:3 ESV) and "Many are the plans in the mind of a man, but it is the purpose of the LORD that will stand" (Proverbs 19:21 ESV). Okay, so planning doesn't mean a lack of trust in the Lord. It's a good thing. But it becomes dangerous when we think we know better than the Lord. So what do we do? We plan to do good, not evil, surround ourselves with wise people who can give us healthy counsel and guidance, create a plan, and hand over those plans to the Lord, knowing God will lead us where He wants us because we know that is the best place to be.

REFLECT

What are you currently planning? Is it for good? Have you received wise counsel and advice? Have you submitted your plans to God with open hands, trusting His way is best?

God of every second, you are the ultimate planner. You planned and put this entire earth together—and everyone on it! Give me guidance and knowledge to plan so that I walk in Your will for my life. Amen.

HE SEES WHAT YOU'RE TRYING TO HIDE

Restore to me the joy of your salvation
and grant me a willing spirit to sustain me.

PSALM 51:12

Relationships can be so hard. There are two ways people relate and communicate today that could drive even the calmest saint up a wall—giant group chats and ghosting in conflict. It's just too hard to keep up in the group chats, am I right? By the time I can look at it, the topic has changed twenty-eight times and I'm completely lost. And then there's "ghosting in conflict." This refers to the act of abruptly ceasing communication with someone during a disagreement, essentially disappearing from their life without explanation. We all know it would be easier to just stop talking about the conflict at hand, pretend it didn't happen, but what does that resolve? If we aren't willing to have the tough conversations, we will miss out on the joy and fellowship that come from having lasting and meaningful relationships.

This is what God wants with us. A lasting, meaningful relationship—one that doesn't go silent when conflict arises, one that doesn't exit the scene when the going gets tough. He wants us to lean in. If we come to God with a heart broken, He will not despise it (Psalm 51:17). We can go to Him with our wrongdoings, and He will forgive them. We can go to Him with our struggles, and He will provide a way. We can go to Him with our pain, and He will comfort us.

King David knew this. He knew he needed God's mercy and compassion. But he also knew he needed to have an honest conversation with God to experience the joy of the Lord he had enjoyed before. We cannot have a thriving relationship with the Lord by walking away when we don't think He will like what we've done, or by neglecting to talk to Him when we feel as if He will be disappointed in us. He sees it all! And He promises to wash it clean as snow. Open up to Him today—don't hide anything back—and experience His peace, freedom, and joy.

REFLECT

Open your hands and hold out anything you keep close to your heart. Ask God for His comfort, guidance, mercy, and forgiveness.

Maker of complete joy, Maker of me, please help me see what I have tried to conceal from you, and help me acknowledge it. Thank You, Lord, for loving me enough to help me grow and cover me in grace. Amen.

LOVE LIKE I LOVE YOU

"When you obey My commandments,
you remain in My love,
just as I obey My Father's commandments
and remain in His love.
I have told you these things
so that you will be filled with My joy.
Yes, your joy will overflow!
This is My commandment:
Love each other in the same way I have loved you."

JOHN 15:10–12 NLT

I ask my toddlers to clean up their playroom before dinner every night. Does it get cleaned? This is me giving you a virtual side-eye. But they try, and at their ages, that's all I'm looking for. One day, my daughter came over to me and asked, "Do you love me because I cleaned up the playroom?" Oof. That question stopped me mid onion chop. I never want her to think that my love for her depends on what she does. But how often do I do something thinking, "This is so God will love me"? Do I love my enemies (Matthew 5:43–45) because of the love Christ has already given me or to gain His approval? Do I gather with other believers (Hebrews 10:24–25) to earn God's love or because He already loves me? What

about caring for those in distress (Matthew 25:34–36) or taking communion (Luke 22:19–20)? We don't uphold His commands to earn His love. We keep His commands because He loves us and so our joy may be complete. All the commands Jesus gave us can be summed up in one command: "Love each other just as I have loved you." How did He love us? It required sacrifice. It was costly. He laid down His life for us, humbly and wholly. Thank You, Jesus.

REFLECT

Loving like Christ and having His joy be complete in us go hand in hand. If joy and God feel far off for you, it may be time to look at your life and see how you love others, especially when things aren't easy. Look at your heart and see if you're trying to earn God's love today or if you're living in His love.

Dear Lord, I want Your joy to be complete in me. Relationships can be tricky, and people can leave at the first sign of discomfort. Help me see where I do this and where I am not loving like Jesus. I want to love better, wholly, and sacrificially. Amen.

NOTHING ABOUT YOU IS A MISTAKE

I praise You because I am fearfully and wonderfully made; Your works are wonderful, I know that full well.

PSALM 139:14

The other day, I met a woman whose kiddo has a disability too, and she told me Psalm 139:14, "I am fearfully and wonderfully made," really bothers her. There would be so many conventional things her child would miss out on. How in the world could God have made her child fearfully and wonderfully?

Fearfully, when translated from Hebrew, means "with great reverence, heartfelt interest, and with respect." *Wonderfully*, when translated from Hebrew, means "unique and set apart." So it's not exactly the way we understand it in English.

We can grieve earthly things we wanted for our children or ourselves that may not happen AND believe they are fearfully and wonderfully made. This is also something to remember about kids who look "typical" on paper. Just because things appear less complex doesn't mean they will partake in every societal milestone or fulfilling role.

Verse 13 of the same psalm, "You knit me together in

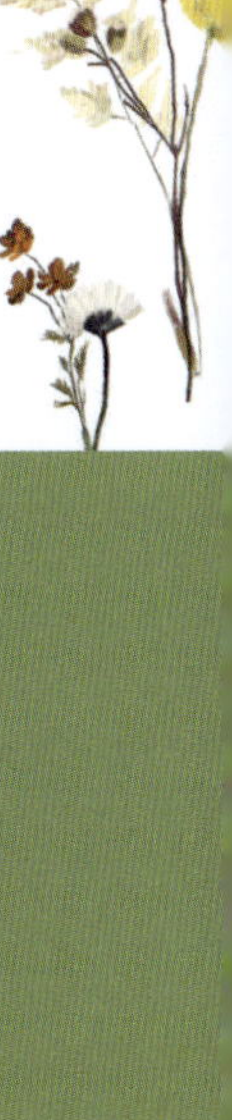

my mother's womb," vividly represents intention. It's a technique. It's slow and steady. It's peaceful and purposeful. The hands that do it must be patient, skilled, and stable. Every person was made with that gravity of intention—fearfully and wonderfully!

When the woman I met looked at me for a response, I paused and told her two things could be true. Like most things in life, it doesn't have to be either/or. You can grieve expectations and dreams you had AND believe your child was intentionally created—fearfully and wonderfully. She smiled at me and said, "That's something to chew on."

REFLECT

Do you treat yourself as one who is fearfully and wonderfully made? Or are the voices of criticism, self-doubt, and insecurity louder? What about someone else in the kingdom of God who has hurt you? What would it take to see them that way too?

Dear God, if I do not treat myself or others like one who is fearfully and wonderfully made, help me with Your Holy Spirit to change that. Amen.

THE ONLY COMPLETE JOY

You make known to me the path of life;
in your presence there is fullness of joy;
at your right hand are pleasures forevermore.

PSALM 16:11 ESV

There's a lot of Scripture in the Bible about how we experience *complete* joy with God—not just joy but a *fullness* of joy. When we're younger, we read Scripture like that and think, "Okay, but will that bring me as much pleasure as a hot husband? Or adorable children? Or jet-setting career opportunities?" But that was when we were younger, right? Because as we grow, we see others put their eggs in these baskets; we witness them searching for their eternal need for joy through other people, new places, and expensive things. But if we think about it, even the most joyous experiences of our lives are fleeting:

- Weddings are said to be the biggest moment in a woman's life. But once she walks down the aisle and the photos are taken and the ceremony is over, marriage doesn't come without valleys.
- Some say holding your newborn baby in your arms for the first time is the closest to pure happiness one

can have. But eventually that moment becomes a beautiful memory. It doesn't last forever.

- Traveling and seeing the world has been said to bring happiness and joy. But when the trip is over, the visit's initial novelty fades with time.

Joy in God's presence doesn't fade. It doesn't become a picture on the wall. It's not just a sweet memory. Jesus Christ is at God's right hand, and when we know Him as our Savior, we are offered pleasure forever. We don't have to worry about the paths of life that will give us the greatest joy, because He does. And not just joy but full, complete joy.

REFLECT

Have you ever experienced the fullness of joy that comes in God's presence? When was the last time? If you have not, ask Him for that today.

Dear Lord, thank You for the path of life You made known to me. I don't want to control my life or put my eggs in a temporary basket. You are who I want to focus on, be with, and trust. Amen.

OVERFLOW WITH HOPE

May the God of hope fill you
with all joy and peace as you trust in Him,
so that you may overflow with hope
by the power of the Holy Spirit.

ROMANS 15:13

When we bought our current home, it was in disarray. The walls were several different colors, red and blue shelves hung on the walls, and water damage sprinkled the floor. But we saw potential, and oh, how lovely that potential looked! Over a couple of years, we've turned this house into a beautiful, peaceful space filled with memories such as my son's first steps and bringing home our baby girl from the NICU. We intended to be here for fifteen, if not twenty years, but then we had our third kiddo, born with Down syndrome, and it hit us that this part of town wasn't the best fit for our family anymore. She needed closer proximity to her school, her therapists, and the hospital, and it meant that the dream home we had created couldn't be ours for much longer. This hasn't been an easy conclusion for us, but after so many honest prayers with the Lord, my husband and I believe the unexplainable peace and joy we have about this decision can only be from the Lord.

When you want an extra serving of joy or peace, the God of hope doesn't hand you a cupful to sip on. He provides you with circumstances to trust and have faith in Him, and you and I will be filled with joy and peace through that belief. We don't know what house or what city we will be in, but we know His plans are best, and I don't have to worry about what tomorrow will bring!

REFLECT

Where has the dust not settled yet, causing you to worry or fear? Is your hope that your life will have joy and peace again once that situation is resolved, or do you live like one who knows you have access to complete joy and peace even in the waiting and unknowing because of hope in Jesus?

Father God, the most powerful joy and peace come from my faith in You rather than my answers. Help me open my hands and say, "I trust You." Let Your Holy Spirit fill me with joy and peace in faith. Your plans are far greater than anything I can imagine. Amen.

NO DROUGHTS THIS SUMMER

But blessed is the one who trusts in the Lord,
whose confidence is in Him.
They will be like a tree planted by the water
that sends out its roots by the stream.
It does not fear when heat comes;
its leaves are always green.
It has no worries in a year of drought
and never fails to bear fruit.

JEREMIAH 17:7–8

Remember a time in your life that just felt easy. You had time to take walks, sit with God, journal your thoughts, and take in the world around you. And then at some point, life sped up on you, and the time you used to spend taking bike rides in the park is now used to do at least ten tasks at once. But as Scripture tells us, if we trust in the Lord and our confidence is in Him, we are like a tree planted by water. We never fail to bear fruit (Galatians 5:22–23) even in a year of drought, because our roots go down to the stream.

What does a drought mean for you? Drought could mean a lack of time or, more so, a lack of being in control of your time. Initially, a lack of control can cause you to worry that you are not as spiritually attuned as you once were.

However, today's Scripture clearly says your faith won't waver if planted by the water. Are you planted in the Lord through spending time with a godly community, reading His Word, praying often, serving His people, and ultimately, walking in hope and joy that comes from faith in Christ? Or are you rarely gathering with God's people, holding your secrets close to your chest, and overall, taking a consumeristic approach to faith? Think about it—even in the busiest seasons of your life, don't you want your leaves to be green? Don't you want to bear all the good fruit—love, joy, peace, patience, kindness, goodness, gentleness, faithfulness, and self-control? If you are with the Lord, you can.

REFLECT

Where are you planted? Who is in your corner helping you be planted there? What rhythms do you have in place to be planted by the water?

Dear Lord, I feel so grateful to know I am blessed by You when I trust in You. Even in the drought and the heat, You are there, giving me all I need. Amen.

DEAR LORD,
EVEN IN THE DROUGHT
AND THE HEAT,
YOU ARE THERE,
GIVING ME
ALL I NEED.

SURRENDERING THE IDEAL TIME

So then, just as you received Christ Jesus as Lord,
continue to live your lives in Him,
rooted and built up in Him,
strengthened in the faith as you were taught,
and overflowing with thankfulness.

COLOSSIANS 2:6–7

Never in my life have I not brushed my teeth twice a day until I had a third kid. Kid number three also taught me there is no "ideal" time to meet with the Lord. I used to set out my colorful pens, put on the right music, have a fresh cup of coffee, and then open my Bible. Now, I probably have yogurt in my hair, children trying to climb me, and an icy cup of coffee. Thank goodness God doesn't require my idea of "ideal," He just wants me. The same applies to you. He just wants you.

It might be singing worship while driving the kids to school, praying while folding laundry, and reading a devo much earlier in the morning before anything else. Your hunger and intention matter more than the ideal circumstance. The ways I spend time with Him have changed this season, but I overflow with thankfulness regardless of circumstance because I continue to live in Him! I get my strength from Him in the mornings and thank Him for another day of caring for

my family in the evenings. To be rooted and built up in Him is an immensely secure feeling. Motherhood feels like worship when He's on my mind in the minutiae. The simple daily prayer, "God, You know the responsibilities I hold. Multiply my time, and help me know You more today," has been one of my favorites in motherhood. Your rhythms might change with your circumstances, but if you're rooted in the Lord and built up in Him, you will be strengthened in your faith no matter your circumstances and overflowing with thankfulness!

REFLECT

When do you spend time with the Lord? What does being rooted and living in Him look like for you? A good measure of whether you are living your life in Him is whether you are strengthened in faith and overflowing with thankfulness. Be honest with yourself here.

Lord Jesus, thank You so much for the strength and thankfulness that comes from being rooted and built up in You. Please help me continue to live my life in You and You alone. Amen.

WE DON'T MOVE IN FEAR

"Therefore do not be anxious about tomorrow,
for tomorrow will be anxious for itself.
Sufficient for the day is its own trouble."

MATTHEW 6:34 ESV

Imagine drinking extra water today so that you don't get thirsty tomorrow. That makes no sense, and you would not do that. We have to drink water daily to reap its benefits and stay healthy. The same is true with training our minds not to be anxious about the future. Matthew 6:34 reminds us that sufficient for the day is its own trouble! Why add heaps of days onto today's plate when that's out of your control and, frankly, out of your capacity? Did you know that in many cases there is a blueprint for anxiety? First, it starts with "WHY is this happening?" Then it adds "HOW can something good come from this?" And finally, "DOES He really care enough to make things change for the better?"

Oh, our tumultuous hearts. It's so easy to think that if we are surprised, He must also be in each disappointment, frustration, or loss. But He isn't—He's all-knowing. Isn't that tremendously comforting?

Why is it comforting?

- Because He knows our past, present, and our future. And all our fears of "What if this happens?" are just that—fears, not the truth of what is to come.
- Because He promises to walk alongside us. Each hurt, disappointment, or closed door is one that He feels with us and is working together for our good—even if we can't see it yet.
- Because He doesn't play by our rules. Do you think a God who created the earth, the moon, the stars, and everything else is scared of what the days will bring? At His whisper, the storms calm, the blind can see, and our lives can radically change.

REFLECT

We don't sit in anxiety, fear, or doubt about tomorrow, because He knows it all. And not only does He know, but He also cares! He is eager to walk with you through it and give you a peace that surpasses all understanding.

Dear Prince of Peace, Knower of All, help me relieve myself of trying to control the future. You know what the future holds. Help me live for today and trust You with my tomorrow. Amen.

THE FORMULA

Do not be anxious about anything,
but in everything by prayer and supplication
with thanksgiving let your requests
be made known to God.
And the peace of God,
which surpasses all understanding,
will guard your hearts and your minds
in Christ Jesus.

PHILIPPIANS 4:6–7 ESV

Growing up, were you more of a math or reading/writing person? If you were a math person, it just made sense to you. There is a formula for every type of problem, so you can figure it out no matter what the equation is. Are there formulas for when life feels out of control? If there is a "formula" for reducing anxiety in the Bible, Philippians 4:6–7 are the verses to focus on. Scripture says rather than be anxious about anything, by prayer and supplication with thanksgiving in everything, let your requests be made known to God so that the peace of God, which surpasses all understanding, will guard your hearts and minds in Christ Jesus.

Let's break it down. Prayer is communication with God. Talk to Him like you are talking to your father or good friend. He's listening. Prayer also includes time to hear what He

says to you. Supplication is a humble pleading or request to God. Prayer doesn't always contain an ask, but supplication does. So, with a humble heart, make your requests known. Thanksgiving is when you express gratitude and praise to God. So come before Him with your prayers, humble requests, and praise so that the peace of God, the most incredible peace you can have, will guard your heart and mind! The peace of God doesn't flood you only when He answers your prayer request. It can flood you even after you make your request known. This peace only comes because of Jesus and is freely offered today.

REFLECT

What storm are you in? Do you think the peace that surpasses all understanding will only come to you once the storm ends, or do you believe you can have that peace even right now in the middle?

Dear Lord, thank You for Your peace that guards my heart and mind in Christ Jesus. Please help me get into a practice of prayer, supplication, and thanksgiving so that I may continuously receive Your peace. Amen.

SURRENDERING FRIENDSHIPS

The righteous choose their friends carefully,
but the way of the wicked leads them astray.

PROVERBS 12:26

Have you ever been surrounded by people yet feel alone? It happens. Even in at your own birthday party, you can feel a lack of connection, as if you have to hide your true self to be accepted. Or maybe the relationships you have are void of depth or meaning and it all feels superficial. If this is you, here are two things you can ask God for:

1. Ask Him to develop deep and healthy friendships that bring you closer to Him.
2. Ask Him to distance you from anyone who will stunt your spiritual growth.

God knows the kind of people we need around us. When we think of friends, we often think of fun or how long we've known someone. But a true friend goes deeper. A true friend is willing to give you heartfelt counsel (Proverbs 27:9) and challenge you (Proverbs 27:17). A true friend has a continued loyalty (II Samuel 1:23), forgiving heart (Colossians 3:13), willingness to sacrifice (John 15:13), obedient spirit (John 15:14), and like-mindedness (Philippians 2:19–23). A true

friend rejoices when you rejoice but also will mourn when you mourn (Romans 12:15).

God will bless you with friends who pray for you, have joy woven throughout their stories even in the most challenging moments, and do not rely on their strength but on the One who made them! It's okay if you didn't start off with these friends. Sometimes you have to grow and learn the significance of the qualities of good friends before you even know what to ask for. It only matters who you are surrounded with today—and if you are feeling alone in your circle, maybe it's time to ask God to intervene.

REFLECT

Do you have any of the above characteristics when you inventory your relationships? Do your friends care for you and spur you on toward the Lord?

Father of all living things, you know when I need companionship. Lord, please help me choose my friends wisely so I can be encouraged, and built up, and grow more in my love and knowledge of You! Help me embody these characteristics for my friends as well. Amen.

THIS SEASON MATTERS

There is a time for everything,
and a season for every activity
under the heavens.

ECCLESIASTES 3:1

Have you ever wanted to press fast-forward on the hard times to get to the good times? Every difficulty has an opportunity to trust God and know Him more and experience His stability, peace, and joy in the middle of it. Is it wrong to want a different season in your life, like one with a slower pace or fewer trials? Not at all. You can absolutely bring that to the Lord.

My husband and I recently discussed wanting to expand our family, but if he has to go through radiation, that may not happen for a long time, if ever. Right now, it does seem like God is saying "no" or "not yet." And while that is hard for me, I need to trust that. Thankfully, He says He will walk with me through it all, and there is grace in the process of surrender. I have no idea what the future holds with our family, but trusting that God's timing and plans are hands down the best helps me be present in the season I am in right now.

"There is a time for everything, and a season for every activity under the heavens." We must remember that while seasons change, God stays the same. He keeps His promises, and our various circumstances are not caused by accident! God orchestrates or allows everything because there is purpose behind it all. I hope that encourages you like it does me to suffer well, endure well, and even rejoice in the Lord in it all!

REFLECT

Is there something you wish was happening right now? Do you trust that there is a season for every activity under the heavens and that God has not forgotten you?

Father God, Your ways are far greater and better than I can ever plan for myself. There is so much freedom in that knowledge! Looking back on my life, I can see You have only been good and always have been with me, even in the most unsure, scary, and unnerving times. Thank You. Amen

THERE IS ENOUGH FOR TODAY

This is the day the LORD has made.
We will rejoice and be glad in it.

PSALM 118:24 NLT

God is so clear that we are meant to live with today on our minds. He tells us not to worry or be anxious about tomorrow because it will bring its own worries (Matthew 6:34). God tells us that there are new mercies every morning so that no matter how difficult the day before was, we can wake up with refreshed hope (Lamentations 3:22–23). He tells us that we can plan, but He directs our paths (Proverbs 16:9). Whether people realize it or not, most anxiety derives from wishing to be like God and know what the future holds.

- Will that job offer come?
- Will that relationship blossom into something?
- Will the diagnosis change?
- Will the prayer be answered?

We don't know, and we rob ourselves of abundant joy offered to us today by fixating on tomorrow. This applies also to exciting moments! When I was getting married, I wanted the months to fly by so I could get to my wedding day. My mom reminded me that anticipation is half the excitement of an event, and there was something to be gained from every day leading up to it. I reminded myself of that in each pregnancy too. Good things come in their own time, and rushing the present means we miss out on this day God made. This day He made has enough for us to rejoice and celebrate in it! Meet Him in the present; that's where He is with you. Yes, God also goes before you, but He's not asking you to meet Him there. He's saying, "This is the day I have made. There is enough for you today."

REFLECT

Is there something you want the answer to that is taking up a lot of your present time? Is there an event coming up that you're fixated on? Where are you not being present or rushing through your day?

God of every minute, nothing is wasted with You. You have packed this day to the brim with purpose and with more than enough for me to rejoice and celebrate. Help me relieve control over wanting to know or have the future come by more quickly. Could You help me be present today? Amen.

APPROVAL IS A SCAM

Am I now trying to win the approval of human beings,
or of God? Or am I trying to please people?
If I were still trying to please people,
I would not be a servant of Christ.

GALATIANS 1:10

I am the best at winning arguments . . . in the shower. Between shampooing and a deep conditioning, I have the quickest comebacks, filled with snappy statements and diligent delivery. But in real life? I'm usually a deer in headlights. In the past, this bothered me because I wished I could defend myself in the moment or be quicker with comebacks, but then I realized I didn't need to defend myself. God does it for me. It's okay when people make incorrect assumptions or describe me inaccurately. Their opinion shouldn't linger with me if they aren't invested in me. If they don't love me, their words don't need to stay longer than when they go in one ear and out the other.

You know who is invested in us and who does love us? Jesus. Oh, He loves us so much. He is so invested in us that He gave His life on the cross. So when He speaks, it behooves us to listen. Paul also strongly reminds us that if we were still trying to please people, we would not be a servant of Christ. And yet, we allow ourselves to be rampant

people pleasers. It's hard to remember that while we want to be liked by peers, do well at work, and be affirmed in our day, we don't need nor should we seek anyone's approval. Take a moment and mentally comb through your week. The way you move, the steps you take, the pictures you share, the words you say—who are you trying to please? The easiest way to stop seeking approval from people is to seek Jesus. He will make all your paths straight and keep you in perfect peace!

REFLECT

Is people-pleasing a problem for you? Whose approval do you seek that is not Jesus?

Jesus, I only want to be Your servant! I do not wish to pine after the approval of friends, family, and strangers. Please help me keep my eyes on You. Please show me where I am seeking the approval of man and help me remove myself from those webs so I can be free to focus on You and You alone! Amen.

THE END IS GUARANTEED

For God so loved the world
that He gave His one and only Son,
that whoever believes in Him
shall not perish but have eternal life.

JOHN 3:16

What's the balance of preparing for the future but living in the present? It's easy to start thinking of life as a steady line that peaks at every milestone—one in which you prepare for months for each milestone moment, and once it happens, you immediately start chasing and planning for the next one. When you live life like this, it can start to feel like you're a kid on the monkey bars, swaying from significant moment to significant moment.

While it is wise to consider the future, it is essential to rejoice today in the day the Lord has made (Psalm 118:24) because not one day is guaranteed for us. We have no control over our next hour, let alone our tomorrow. Heaven is the only guarantee in this life. And if we are always picturing the next big thing, planning for the next monumental moment, daydreaming about the day of "insert milestone," we are missing what God has designed for us today! And how sad is that! He is present and with us in the mundane if only we'd slow down to listen and witness. The truth is, the only certain plan you can have is to focus on heaven. That end is guaranteed thanks to the salvation you have in believing in Jesus Christ. Let the truth of John 3:16 permeate into your heart. What a relief.

REFLECT

Are you someone who lives mainly in the present? Do you find yourself daydreaming more about the past or the future?

Father God, thank You so much for this day. Today is filled with an agenda You have for me. If only I would slow down to see it. Please give me Your eyes so that I don't miss it. Please provide me with the pace so I don't walk past it. Help my heart value the ordinary, because You are just as present there as You are in the monumental moments. Amen.

IT ALL WORKS TOGETHER FOR GOOD

And we know that for those who love God
all things work together for good,
for those who are called according to his purpose.

ROMANS 8:28 ESV

When my daughter's audiologist brought in a chart showing me where her hearing registered and pointed between a lawnmower and a roaring airplane, I lost it. We had an inkling that she might have hearing loss but did not realize she was profoundly deaf. Besides worrying about how this would affect her communication, social skills, and ability to be understood by peers, my initial question was, "Why, God? Why would you take this from her or allow it to happen?" We went through all the emotions from denial, anger, sadness, numbness, and acceptance to finally peace.

What brought about this lasting peace? Remembering who was in control and who was not surprised by this news. Remembering that yes, we love God, and according to the inerrant truth of Romans 8:28, "all things work together for good for those who are called according to his purpose." God's good doesn't mean a life of ease or prosperity. It doesn't mean comfort or lack of aches. There are many aches and pains in life, but God's good plans are to make

us look more like Christ! The pain from suffering is valid, but know it isn't in vain. Sometimes, we cannot see "the why" until much later, if ever, and occasionally, by His grace, He lets us see why. I can wholeheartedly tell you I've seen Him working for our good. Our family is closer. We are learning the beautiful language of ASL (American Sign Language). We are learning to worship in new ways. In moments, it can be hard. But it is all so, so good, just like our God.

REFLECT

Do you love God? If so, do you believe He works everything together for your good? What is keeping you from thinking that? Is it an unseen resolution, unanswered prayers, or was it being told "no"?

God of all that is good, thank You today for the ways You've worked all things for my good whether I see it yet or not. Thank You for telling me no sometimes. Thank You for the doors You've opened. Thank You for being my Shepherd and never leaving me, no matter the situation. Amen.

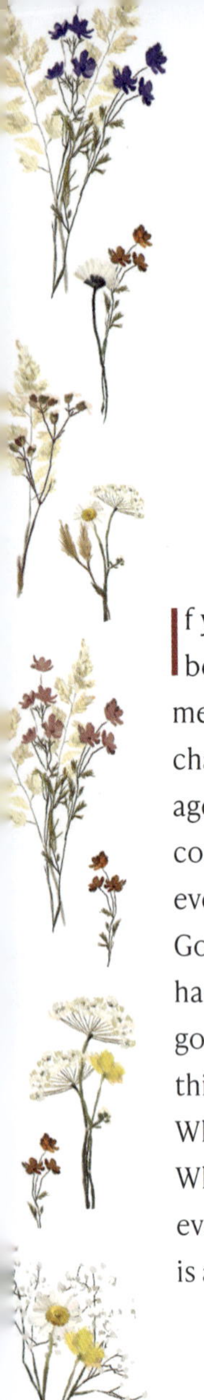

UNCHANGING GOD, CONSTANTLY CHANGING PEOPLE

But the fruit of the Spirit is love, joy, peace, forbearance, kindness, goodness, faithfulness, gentleness and self-control.

GALATIANS 5:22–23

If you met up with yourself from ten years ago, would you be looking at the same person you see today? I don't mean those lovely laugh lines or the wise grays; would your character, strengths, and maturity be identical to ten years ago? What about twenty? If you have the Holy Spirit and are constantly being made to be more like Jesus, you likely aren't even the same person you were six months ago. But God is. God has been the same from the beginning (Malachi 3:6). He has always had the most love, joy, peace, patience, kindness, goodness, faithfulness, gentleness, and self-control. And this unchanging God asks us to trust Him (Proverbs 3:5–6). Who better is there to trust? Who has more qualifications? Who is more worthy of our surrender of control? No one. In every anxiety, He knows what is to come. In every shock, He is a firm foundation.

Change is constant in our lives, but God is never sur-

prised by life. He never spends His time pacing back and forth, worried or fearful. I'm sure you can see how this world is changing. But instead of moving left and right like the wind with all the change, we stay focused on Yahweh, the Unchanging One, and ask for His Spirit to guide us in all circumstances. If He does not change your circumstances, He will change your heart.

Unchanging, perfect God, thank You for how You mold me to be more like Jesus. By Your grace alone, I have the Holy Spirit and can say I am not the same as I was. Please continue Your work in me so I may be perfect and lacking in nothing (James 1:4). Amen.

REFLECT

Where have you seen yourself change in the last decade consistent with the fruit of the Spirit (love, joy, peace, patience, kindness, gentleness, goodness, faithfulness, and self-control)? Have you been more loving? Have you experienced more joy and peace? Go through each fruit and ask yourself if you see this characteristic growing in you. And if so, give God thanks for that today. If not, ask Him for more of that fruit today.

GOD IS
NEVER
SURPRISED
BY LIFE.

WHO IS HE?

In his hand is the life of every living thing
and the breath of all mankind.

JOB 12:10 ESV

Does the fact that God holds our lives and breath in His hands comfort or scare you? Let's examine who God is.

- God is self-sufficient (John 5:26). He doesn't need a thing from you or me! He will never run out on us. What a mercy.
- God is all-powerful (Psalm 33:6). If opening your hands and surrendering control seems daunting, knowing God is all-powerful should bring you peace! He can handle it all.
- God is everywhere (Psalm 139:7–10). God isn't too busy with one person or on one side of the world that He will forget you. While we cannot be everywhere all at once, He can.
- God is all-knowing (Isaiah 46:9–10). He doesn't have to look at a crystal ball, cards, or the stars to know what is happening.
- God is perfectly wise (Romans 11:33). He sees every thought behind the words. He understands all the grids of human relationships and beyond. God knows the impact of every action and the ripple effects.

- God is perfectly faithful (II Timothy 2:13). To those who love Him, He works all things together for their good.
- God is perfectly just (Deuteronomy 32:4). He will never let evil win in the grand scheme of eternity.
- God never changes (Malachi 3:6). There is so much comfort in knowing that all these characteristics are who God is for eternity!
- God is love (I John 4:7–8). He is the best Father. So, while He holds the life and breath of every living thing, we can rest knowing He will only move in ways that are in love because He is love.

REFLECT

Do you live your life like one who knows that there is only One who controls the life and breath of every living thing? Does that bring you freedom or fear?

Lord, You are in control from when I wake up to when I go to sleep, so I open my hands and trust You with my life. Amen.

BE ROOTED HERE

For I know the plans I have for you,
declares the LORD, plans for welfare and not for evil,
to give you a future and a hope.

JEREMIAH 29:11 ESV

Are you building your life where you are? Or are you waiting for something to happen before you can be present? What if God wants you to be rooted where you are today? Picture this–you are moving to a whole different city in a few months. Currently, you are deep in the in-between. Boxes are packed and stacked, and your closet is a suitcase. You don't know when your house will sell, when you will be moving, or where exactly you are moving to, so do you continue to build connections in the city where you currently live? Or do you keep to yourself and wait it out, thinking, *What's the use?* Let's dive into Jeremiah 29.

This passage is an excellent reminder to trust God's timing and be rooted where we are today. Jeremiah tells the weary, wailing, and worn-out exiles of Babylon that God wants them to build homes and live peacefully, even in captivity. He expresses the importance of ignoring and denying the false prophets who wish their timelines to be the truth rather than God's. He assures them that God has their interest in mind. Not only is the Lord invested in them, but God's plans for the exiles are crystal clear, "plans for welfare and not for evil, to give you a future and a hope." God has not forgotten them, and they are not an afterthought. He is with them, and He is with you. The in-between is a holy time with much to do! There is fruit to bear, there are people to love, and there are opportunities to share God's grace. This day isn't pointless. You can plant right where you are and let your roots deepen for however long you are here.

REFLECT

Where are you in the "in-between" in your life? Do you trust that you can be here now without having all the answers in your hand?

God of every second of every day, You have me here today for a reason. I pray You would open my eyes and show me who to love and care for. Help me deepen my roots as I walk through this day. Amen.

HE DOES GIVE YOU MORE THAN YOU CAN HANDLE

No temptation has overtaken you
that is not common to man. God is faithful,
and he will not let you be tempted beyond your ability,
but with the temptation he will also provide the way
of escape, that you may be able to endure it.

1 CORINTHIANS 10:13 ESV

After I got my daughter's hard of hearing diagnosis, so many people said to me, "God only gives you what you can handle." I know they meant well, but I did not feel like I could handle another diagnosis on my own. It felt overwhelming, unfair, and inaccurate to believe that God gave me this because He thought I could "handle" it. The reality is that statement is missing the most essential part. God only gives you what you can handle WITH HIM. Scripture tells us that while we may be tempted or have trials that challenge us, WITH GOD, it will not be beyond us to escape or endure it. God has the power to hold our hands and carry us through. We saw the Lord do this with the Red Sea. We saw this with the immense patience of Zechariah and Elizabeth waiting on a child. We saw this most of all

with Jesus on the cross. So the next time you find yourself in a situation where you are sorely tempted or deeply challenged, it is okay to know and acknowledge that you cannot do this alone.

Contrary to what popular philosophies like to peddle, you are not enough. But do you know who is? The Lord your God. He is the most powerful. The most knowledgeable. The most just. The most loving. Your God will never leave you or forsake you. As you encounter all that is "common to man," rest in the confidence that He will always fight your battles with you.

REFLECT

Through faith in the Lord, people from before and after you will endure. Where do you need to trust and believe that God will be with you as you endure today?

Lord of my days, I open my hands to the trials in my life that feel like too much. I praise You that You are always with me. Help me believe that when I feel burdened, alone, and tired, Your mighty hand is gripping tight to mine, not letting go. Amen.

SURRENDER THE TEARS

Those who sow in tears
shall reap with shouts of joy!
He who goes out weeping,
bearing the seed for sowing,
shall come home with shouts of joy,
bringing his sheaves with him.

PSALM 126:5–6 ESV

As kids, many of us were taught not to cry. It would start innocently enough. We'd scrape our knee or fall, and while we were getting tended to, we'd hear, "Don't cry." The phrase would go on to be repeated after sad movies, being picked up from a hard day at school, losing a tournament, and even when dealing with difficult friendships. "Don't cry" was used many times in my childhood by many well-meaning, truly caring people. But, as children, the message that comes with this phrase is that crying and sadness is a deficiency that should be hidden. But so much Scripture shows us how sadness is an emotion where we can depend on God and gain power from Him, because sadness isn't the end of the Christian's story. Joyful shouts. Mercies. All will be right again. So sadness isn't a disadvantage.

But when was the appropriate time for sadness when I

had things to do during the day? Should I compartmentalize it? We can take a look at Psalm 126 for this. While we might be tempted to sit in our sadness and put everything else aside, we must continue with the work set for the day. Whether that's a conference call or a grocery run, we can take our sadness with us, understanding that God knows our hearts and doesn't expect us to dry our faces to carry on with our days. We don't need people's approval to our left or right. We don't need to put on a facade. We can trust that this storyline ends with shouts of joy and that our tears are part of getting us there.

REFLECT

What are you sad about today? Has there been any sadness you've ignored that you need to address today?

God of my life, You hold the world in Your hands. You know when I laugh and when I weep. Please help me surrender to You in moments or seasons of sadness and trust the power of Your Holy Spirit to sustain me. Help me trust that I will shout joyfully at the end of all this. Amen.

A DAY BURSTING WITH PURPOSE

For we are God's handiwork,
created in Christ Jesus to do good works,
which God prepared in advance for us to do.

EPHESIANS 2:10

Do you wake up and look at your day as something to get through? Or do you get excited thinking about the day God has planned for you? From the people you speak with to your time at work, God knows what today brings for you. God's plans for your day, paired with Jesus defeating death on the cross, mean something huge for you today. This day that you are living is ripe with triumphant purpose. This day is bursting with jubilant opportunities. You are here and now by no coincidence. This day the Lord has made is not an accident.

What if you put on this mindset as you started your day and reminded yourself of this? Nothing about the day would feel useless, not even the mundane tasks. You are a victor who isn't defined by her to-do list. Every hour has intention, whether attending a board meeting or loading the dishwasher. You are a recipient of grace who can call on the Holy Spirit for help any time and however often

you need. Fear, worry, and other distractions will try their hardest to keep you from reveling in the day God has for you. But you are a daughter of the highest King, going into each hour striding with purpose. Say it with me, "I am God's handiwork, created in Christ Jesus to do good works, which God prepared in advance for me to do!"

REFLECT

Do you put on this mindset on a day-to-day basis? If not, what can you do to make sure you remember that there is intention, work, and purpose in this day? You could write it on a sticky note and keep it on your mirror, or set a reminder on your phone to reflect on this truth.

Dear Lord, thank You so much for this day You have made. You make nothing by accident and nothing without purpose. Please help me remember this daily, especially in the difficult or the mundane. Please help me do the good works You've created in advance for me to do! Amen.

SEARCH ME, GOD

Search me, God, and know my heart;
test me and know my anxious thoughts.
See if there is any offensive way in me,
and lead me in the way everlasting.

PSALM 139:23–24

Hand it over to me, please," I asked my son for the third time. He zipped around the corner, scissors in hand, and refused to turn over his newest toy. Maybe it was because he thought he knew better. Maybe it was because he enjoyed the thrill of rebelling. Maybe it was because he was worried I would react with a consequence. Yes, I think it was the third one because when I said, "I am not angry at you. Please give me the scissors before you hurt yourself or your sister," he sheepishly dropped them two feet in front of me (of course) and ran away screaming, "I'm sorry!"

Toddlers. They are a whole other breed of chaos. But then I think about myself and can't help but ask, how often do I run around with my own "scissors" and fight to keep them to myself? I think I can handle it; I know better, and maybe if I'm really honest with myself, I am worried about what God will think if I tell Him I'm holding onto it. But He already knows. And He loves me still. David's words in Psalm 139 strike me to my core when I remember that God is the only one who can make my heart clean, more like Jesus, and also lead me to the everlasting place. Nothing of this world will lead me to that place of complete love, the path that brings us back to Him. God is not waiting to punish you or criticize you. He is here to make you more like His perfect, holy Son and surround you in love while doing so.

REFLECT

What keeps you from asking God to search your heart? Do you trust that He alone can lead you in the way that is everlasting?

Father God, we boldly and trustfully pray this Scripture over our day. Seach us, O Lord! Do a work in us, O Lord! Please don't leave us to ourselves and our devices and vices. Help us be more like your perfect and holy Son, Jesus. Amen.

HIS TIMING IS ALWAYS RIGHT

But the angel said to him:
"Do not be afraid, Zechariah;
your prayer has been heard.
Your wife Elizabeth will bear you a son,
and you are to call him John."

LUKE 1:13

When unbelievers are asked what keeps them from trusting God most, they usually say, "God didn't answer my prayer." Unanswered prayers can be disappointing and leave us feeling hopeless. But then I remember Zechariah and Elizabeth—two of the most faithful people to love the Lord. Scripture says, "Both of them were righteous in the sight of God, observing all the Lord's commands and decrees blamelessly. But they were childless because Elizabeth was not able to conceive, and they were both very old" (Luke 1:6-7). When it looked like parenthood might not be a part of their journey, it would have been so easy for Zechariah and Elizabeth to waver or walk away. Yet, they pressed on. They ached for a child. They prayed ceaselessly for one even when Elizabeth was well past childbearing years. And even though person after person near them likely had baby after baby, they continued

to serve God and His people and trust that He loved and cared for them more than they could imagine.

The life of Zechariah and Elizabeth always reminds me that God's *yes* might come decades after I thought it was "the right time." Can you imagine how they reacted when one day, "the angel said to him: 'Do not be afraid, Zechariah; your prayer has been heard. Your wife Elizabeth will bear you a son, and you are to call him John'? God's timing is better than ours. God's plans are better than our own. If He says *yes* to us on a timeline of what we expect, that is incredible. If He says *yes* to us at an unexpected time, that is just as miraculous. If He never says *yes* to that request, we must trust that it is for our best.

REFLECT

If you kept asking and God didn't say yes, *would you still call Him faithful? When was a time that God said* yes *that surprised you? Praise Him for the ways He's answered prayers in your life.*

God, any rejection from You is a gift. Any redirection from You is a blessing. Help me release my timelines to You and open my hands to the plans You have for me every day. Amen.

UNEXPECTED HEALING

When she heard about Jesus,
she came up behind him in the crowd
and touched His cloak, because she thought,
"If I just touch His clothes, I will be healed."
Immediately her bleeding stopped and she felt
in her body that she was freed from her suffering.

MARK 5:27–29

The cashier handed me the last items she scanned, and I was surprised to see Pringles. I raised my eyebrow at my daughter, and she said, "I need this snack, Mom!!" The cashier laughed, and honestly, I was amused enough to buy the Pringles. But you can believe we talked about the need to transparently ask Mom instead of being sneaky once we got in line. I reminded her that Mom loves her and wants to give her what she can! Of course, this made me think of my relationship with Jesus.

Do I trust Him with every need that I have? Or do I try to be near Him just when I want something? The latter makes me think of the woman who had been bleeding for twelve years. Think about where you were in life twelve years ago. Can you imagine having that condition that long? Several doctors failed her, and her condition only got worse after she sought help! She felt cut off from society and God, so Jesus was her last attempt. Even in her pain and her

loneliness, she believed that just a touch of Jesus's robes as He walked by her would cure her dreadful, desolate condition. She was at the end of her rope and had nothing to lose. She pushed through the jostling crowd, lifted her hand to brush His robes, and was instantly healed. Can you imagine the relief she felt? That is what He offers you and me today.

REFLECT

Where in your life today do you have a sense of empathy with this woman? It could be a chronic condition, a longstanding pain, a deep loneliness, or something else. Bring it before God with confidence.

Jesus, You stopped to see the woman who desperately reached for Your robe. You heard her after her years of suffering, and You healed her. You know where I sit in a similar situation. Please, listen to me today, Lord! Heal me, make a way, and give me strength to faithfully endure. Amen.

COME TO HIM MORE THAN WHEN YOU WANT

At once Jesus realized that power had gone out
from Him. He turned around in the crowd and asked,
"Who touched My clothes?"
"You see the people crowding against You,"
His disciples answered, "and yet You can ask,
'Who touched Me?'" But Jesus kept looking around
to see who had done it. Then the woman,
knowing what had happened to her,
came and fell at His feet and, trembling with fear,
told Him the whole truth. He said to her,
"Daughter, your faith has healed you.
Go in peace and be freed from your suffering."

MARK 5:30–34

Often, we read the story of the woman who had been bleeding for twelve years and was healed by the touch of Jesus's robes, and we stop there. We say, "Ah, Jesus healed her, hallelujah!" But the second part of this story is just as important. After she was healed, she had no plans to reveal herself. But Scripture tells us that Jesus felt power leave Him and asked, "Who touched Me?" Why did Jesus do that? Usually, He is more anonymous in the ways

He cares for people. But Jesus wanted her to know that yes, while He can heal her (and He did), He also is more than His provision. Her confession is a powerful testimony for all who knew her condition, and her faith was made stronger in acknowledging our Lord for who He is. He met her needs, and she declared His glory. God wants to make our faith perfect and lacking in nothing. What a grace that even while Jesus was on the way to another place where people frantically needed His help, He took the time to heal this woman, have her confess, and strengthen her faith.

REFLECT

When you are in need, whether it's a chronic condition like this woman or something else, do you come to Jesus transparently? Do you declare His glory when He does answer your prayers?

Dear Lord, You are so good to me. Today, I come before You to ask about these needs of mine, and I trust that You will help me. I don't want to only be around You when I want or need something. Give me the boldness to declare Your glory in how you've blessed me! You are my good, good God, and I am a living testimony of Your grace. Amen.

AM I MAKING A DIFFERENCE HERE?

He said to me, "You are My servant,
Israel, and you will bring Me glory."
I replied, "But my work seems so useless!
I have spent my strength for nothing and
to no purpose. Yet I leave it all in the LORD's hand;
I will trust God for my reward."

ISAIAH 49:3–4 NLT

Have you ever had days where you wondered if what you're doing here on earth is making a difference? Please tell me I'm not the only one. Yes, I know raising my children is an incredible calling and generational work. Yes, I understand I bring the Lord glory through raising and caring for them. But some days, it feels pretty fruitless between the diapers and the doodles, the macaroni and the messes. I look to my left and hear her podcast hitting it out of the park, and I look to my right and see her write yet another bestseller. Looking straight ahead in the mirror, I wonder if there is any work I'm doing here that's good.

On days like this, where comparison is croaking away and strength feels shallow, the Holy Spirit reminds me of Isaiah. Even the unswervingly faithful prophet of God felt like how he spent his strength and his work was "useless." How

do we know that? Because he was so honest with the Lord. He wrestled with Him. He bared his emotions to Him. And yet, he always trusted Him. Isaiah gives us a roadmap of how to be faithful and be in a close, dependent, trusting relationship with the Lord, even in challenging situations. Let go of thinking you can't wrestle with our loving, all-knowing Creator. Let go of thinking you're the only one whose work feels useless sometimes. Bare it to our good God and leave it all in the Lord's hands.

REFLECT

Which part is more difficult for you: wrestling honestly with God or being able to say, "Yet I leave it all in the Lord's hand; I will trust God for my reward"?

O God, You know what situation came to mind when I read this devotional. Please help me spend some time transparently bringing it to You—totally, honestly, fully. Amen.

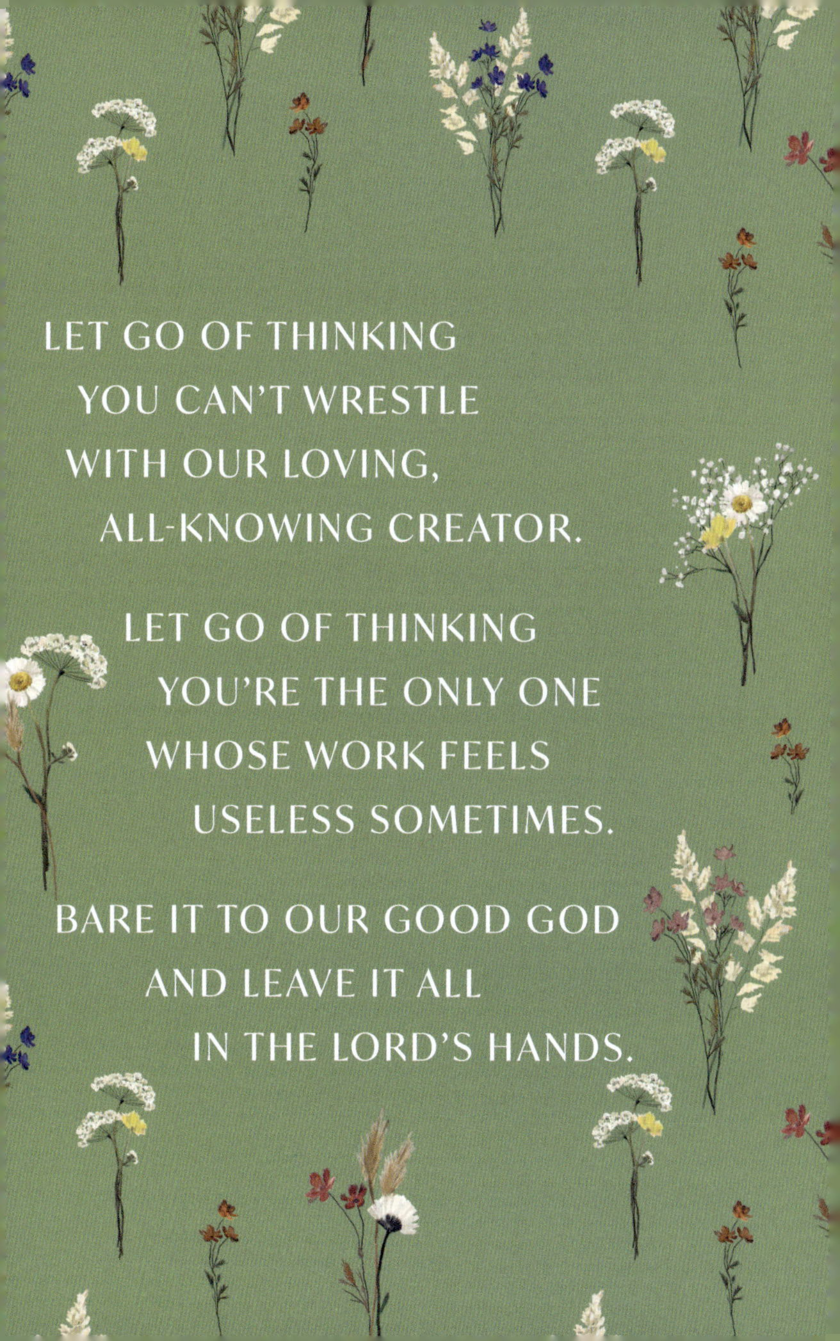
LET GO OF THINKING
YOU CAN'T WRESTLE
WITH OUR LOVING,
ALL-KNOWING CREATOR.
LET GO OF THINKING
YOU'RE THE ONLY ONE
WHOSE WORK FEELS
USELESS SOMETIMES.
BARE IT TO OUR GOOD GOD
AND LEAVE IT ALL
IN THE LORD'S HANDS.

SAME STRUGGLES, DIFFERENT SCENARIOS

And your ears shall hear a word behind you,
saying, "This is the way, walk in it,"
when you turn to the right or when you turn to the left.

ISAIAH 30:21 ESV

Do you remember being a dramatic, angsty teenager, walking around in your green high-tops while listening to Breaking Benjamin and writing lists about everything wrong in life, such as:

- I didn't get an officer position. Now, I won't get into college. Way to fail.
- My crush didn't smile at me in the hallway. Will anyone ever notice me?

Don't you wish you could have advised your younger self that when life doesn't go the way you imagine it, it usually means you are being redirected or protected because you have a good God?

We often look back and wonder why we just couldn't learn that lesson sooner. But what about today? Are you in a situation today that you will be looking back on in ten or fifteen years and wondering why you held on to every single detail? Maybe today's list looks more like:

- I didn't get the promotion I wanted at work. I feel embarrassed and so disappointed.

To more serious ones.

- I am so overwhelmed with the fact that our youngest child is deaf. Am I going to fail her?

It's easy to look back and tell our younger selves how to act, but we often still struggle with the same things. The intensity of our worries may have increased, but the root is the same—a lack of trust in God's ability to use adversity, discomfort, and rejection for our good and His glory. Even when we're at fault! He will never leave us. What an incredible reminder today. He is with us in our shortcomings. He is with us when the challenge seems too great.

REFLECT

Where is God telling you to walk His ways in faith today?

God of mercy and grace, decades have passed, and I still struggle to trust the way You have before me. Today, I surrender my worries and fears to You. Please give me the peace and patience the Holy Spirit offers and be near to the troubles in my heart. Amen.

IN THE MOUNTAINS AND THE VALLEYS

The LORD your God is in your midst,
a mighty one who will save;
he will rejoice over you with gladness;
he will quiet you by his love;
he will exult over you with loud singing.

ZEPHANIAH 3:17 ESV

My daughter was the kind of baby who wanted Dad for all things fun until she felt sick or hurt herself. Did I wish she also wanted to spend time with me when she wanted to delight in a fun toy or sunshine outside? Absolutely. As she's gotten older, she's learned to see me as someone to go to for fun and good moments, and I'm grateful for that! But initially, it was hard to be wanted solely for what felt like caretaking moments. It also made me curious if I see God that way.

When I look back at the most challenging moments in my life, I see that is when my prayer life is booming, worship music is on repeat, and Scripture is at the tip of my tongue. But in days of ease, my Bible can get a little dusty. To grow in any deep relationship, you spend time with that person in both the good and the difficult moments. Think about your best friend or your spouse. Do you only talk to them when

things are hard? No! You rejoice together, and you mourn together. God is no different. When my child is joyful, I run to receive her joy and multiply it. When my child is in pain, I run to hold her in my arms and comfort her. And I am an imperfect person. God is perfect. He rejoices over us (Zephaniah 3:17), and He is near to the brokenhearted (Psalm 34:18). We serve a mighty God who doesn't want our primary source of joy and comfort to be through things of this world. He desires us to find it in Him! So run to Him today, whether for rejoicing or mourning; run to your good Father! He has joy because He is joy. He has hope because He is hope.

REFLECT

Do you find yourself running to God more in the valley surrounded by challenges or on the mountaintop when life is going well? Why is that?

Dear Lord, You are the God who weeps with us and sings over us in delight. Please help me remember that today and all my days as I encounter more challenges and joys. You are worthy of my attention in it all! Amen.

ABIDING ISN'T A TO-DO ITEM

"I am the vine; you are the branches.
Whoever abides in me and I in him,
he it is that bears much fruit,
for apart from me you can do nothing."

JOHN 15:5 ESV

When was the last time you went a few days without drinking water? I know you forty-ounce tumbler folks are like, "Who skips water?" You're correct that water is essential for us to live. Our bodies can't preserve water today for use tomorrow, so we need a renewed supply daily. Without daily water intake, you're looking at dehydration, which can cause unclear thinking, mood shifts, and failing body functions. I can't think of a more accurate comparison to the necessity and significance of meeting with Jesus daily. John 15:5 is bold in telling us, "Whoever abides in me and I in him, he it is that bears much fruit, for apart from me you can do nothing."

What can we do if we don't abide in Jesus? Nothing. Wait, is this telling you that once you have a quiet time at 8:15 a.m., you've abided enough in Jesus for the rest of the day? Does one large sip of water in the morning keep you hydrated all day? When we read about abiding in Christ,

it means to center our lives around Christ. Yes, we should spend time with Him, but we also meet with and serve His people, pray often, read Scripture, and live our lives in a way that depends on Him like a branch does with a vine. Do you abide in Him daily? When you abide in Christ, your life flourishes spiritually—you will become more Christ-like in character (Galatians 5:22–23), you will notice less anxiety (Philippians 4:6–7), feel closer to and cared for by your Father (I Peter 5:6–7). How can you abide more in Christ today?

REFLECT

What does abiding in Christ look like for you? Is it a monthly, weekly, daily, or hourly practice? How can you increase the ways you abide in Jesus today?

Lord, even when I am tired, even when I need to work late, and even when it feels like my to-do list is piling up, help me abide in You because apart from You, I can do nothing. Amen.

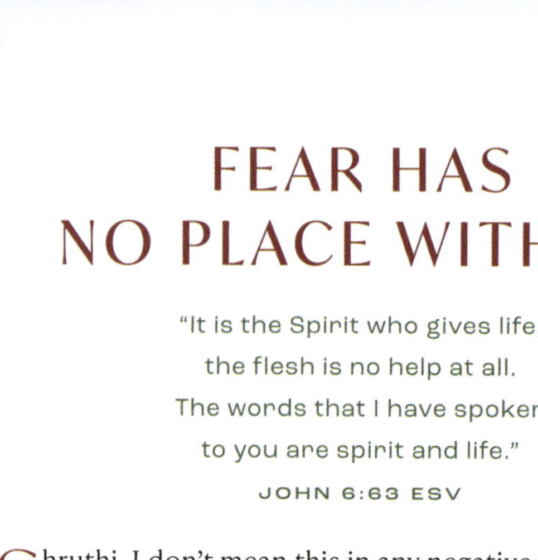

FEAR HAS NO PLACE WITH US

"It is the Spirit who gives life;
the flesh is no help at all.
The words that I have spoken
to you are spirit and life."

JOHN 6:63 ESV

"Shruthi, I don't mean this in any negative way, but I want to know why you didn't terminate your pregnancy after you first got your daughter's Down syndrome diagnosis?" One of the most incredible comforts in knowing Jesus is that we don't make moves in fear. Fear can come close to you; it might even think it has you cornered, but fear has no actual grip on us who abide in Christ. It wants us to forsake our faith and run around in paths of panic. It wants you to lose sight of the fact that there is a faithful and just God who works everything together for your good. Fear wants you to ruminate, hesitate, and deteriorate.

The number of people who asked me that question in the first line of this page would surprise you, but more than being offended, I was heartbroken to see them living in such bottomless fear. Either we believe God will never forsake us as the Scripture says and will always make a way, as He did with the Israelites coming out of Egypt and Christ on the cross, or we don't. Not only do we not make decisions out of fear, but we also have access to the Holy Spirit, who can give us the fruit of the Spirit (including peace, faithfulness, and goodness) in any circumstance. How? By dwelling in the Holy Spirit through the words of Christ. Jesus says, "It is the Spirit who gives life; the flesh is no help at all. The words that I have spoken to you are spirit and life" (John 6:63). So dwell in Christ's words, friend! It is not simply a discipline in the Christian's life. When fear is chasing you down and roaring in your ears, reading our Bibles could make the difference between life and death.

REFLECT

What role does fear play in your day-to-day decisions? Is it a significant motivator, a mediocre meddler, or a stranger you let pass through but not stay for a visit?

Lord, I don't want to waste a single second of my day in a filter of fear. Help me, through Your Holy Spirit, to live with peace, faithfulness, and goodness no matter what comes my way. Help me trust that You are with me and will never forsake me. Amen.

GOD IS NEVER EARLY OR LATE

With the Lord a day is like a thousand years, and a thousand years are like a day.

II PETER 3:8

Imagine showing up everywhere, always at the perfect time. You never have to sit in your car because you get there too early. You never get stuck in traffic. You never run ten minutes behind. We know that would never happen for anyone on this earth, but it does for God. Our mighty Creator is not at the mercy of time, because He constructed time. With the Lord, a day is like a thousand years, and a thousand years are like a day (II Peter 3:8).

God's timing is perfect, and we know that. We've likely said that to encourage our friends. But if we lived in a way that accepted this, we would never be in a rush. We would never think an opportunity has passed us by or God is holding out on us. We would live in patience and peace, waiting on God's perfect timing and meditating on His promises. When impatience in your circumstances arises, remember, "The Lord is not slow in keeping His promise, as some understand slowness" (II Peter 3:9), and a man's heart plans his way, But the Lord directs his steps (Proverbs

16:9). In the meantime, He tells us what to do throughout Scripture. Live holy and godly lives (II Peter 3:11), make every effort to be found spotless, blameless, and at peace with Him (II Peter 3:14), be on your guard so that you may not be carried away by the error of the lawless (II Peter 3:17), and lastly, grow in the grace and knowledge of our Lord and Savior Jesus Christ (II Peter 3:18). Wait on Him.

REFLECT

Where do you not believe that God's time was or is perfect in your life? Release that to Him today.

God of creation, You have been here since before the beginning of time. You are not holding out on me. You have the best timing. Help me, please, believe that in my heart and let that show through my worship, prayers, and actions. Holy Spirit, come and help me release so that I can ultimately grow in the grace and knowledge of Jesus.

THE MOTHER OF MOSES

When she could hide him no longer,
she took for him a basket made of bulrushes
and daubed it with bitumen and pitch.
She put the child in it and placed it
among the reeds by the river bank.

EXODUS 2:3 ESV

Do you know who Jochebed is? She was Moses's mom. She had a few kids, and Moses was born when Pharaoh decreed that any newborn Jewish baby boy was to be thrown into the Nile because he was trying to control the growth and strength of the Israelites (Exodus 1:22). Can you imagine the sheer terror she lived in when she was pregnant, wondering if she was carrying a boy? Then, when he was born, keeping him alive for three months until she finally had to give him up (Exodus 2:3)? Jochebed didn't throw him into the Nile. Instead, she put him in a basket, and Pharaoh's own daughter found Moses. She took pity on the crying baby and, in an incredible turn of events, hired Moses's mom to nurse him.

Can you imagine the faith it took for Jochebed to release Moses from her home because her family risked being exposed by hiding a baby, coming home heartbroken

to an empty crib, only to be then called in by the princess to be paid to care for your own son? The way Jochebed opened her hands and trusted God when everything felt like it was going wrong and she would lose her child are inspiring. God didn't just let her see her son again. He had her be the one who cared for him in those precious newborn days until he grew older (Exodus 2:8–10). She was able to spend that special time heart-to-heart with her son. And God did that for Jochebed. So often, we read about Moses, but he would not even be here if it weren't for his mother's bravery, faith, and surrender.

REFLECT

Where does it seem like you are releasing your basket on the Nile? Know that God sees it, and He is with you.

Dear Lord, thank You for the immense mercies You bless us with that leave us in awe. I pray that whatever I'm holding close and unable to let go of, no matter how precious, I can give to You without hesitation. Please help me open these hands to You like Jochebed did, Lord! Amen.

HIS WAYS ARE HIGHER

"For My thoughts are not your thoughts,
neither are your ways My ways," declares the Lord.
"As the heavens are higher than the earth,
so are My ways higher than your ways
and My thoughts than your thoughts."

ISAIAH 55:8–9

I gently waved my right hand up and down while my left fist rested on my right hand. He raised his eyebrow and asked me, "What does that mean?" "Fart," I told him through my laughter. After finding out our littlest one is hard of hearing, my husband and I started learning ASL. Is it daunting to learn on top of everything we already have on our plate, like raising three kids, running a couple of businesses, and trying to stay in healthy rhythms? Yes. Do I see God moving in incredible ways that bring me to awe? Absolutely. Am I still overwhelmed that life is going far differently than I imagined? Yes.

Thankfully, I'm in good company. Think about sweet Mary, the mother of Jesus. She was engaged to be married. If you're married, do you remember those days? You're giddy, wistful, impatient. She likely daydreamed about her wedding day and future kids. Instead, she received the bless-

ing, and probably the shock, of a lifetime when she was told that she would conceive and carry the Son of God. Can you imagine? There is no way she could have planned for that to happen. She was told not to be afraid, and Mary moved forward in faith. Think about King David and his tumultuous journey to becoming king. Think about Zechariah and Elizabeth and their long journey to parenthood. God never forgot them.

When I learned my daughter was legally deaf, these types of reminders were a balm to my soul. His plans have always been good, His promises have always been true, and from David to Mary, this rings true for me and you. He knows and sees it all! We can't see all the moving parts, but we know whose hand is moving. Rejoice in that today, friend. Anything that doesn't feel like it's going according to plan, undoubtedly is.

REFLECT

Where do you need to open your hands? Where do you need to trust His plan?

Not even a wave in the water moves without Your knowledge, Lord. I want Your plans to be the plans I want for my life. Please help me continue to open my hands and trust You. Amen.

HE IS OUR VICTOR

> The Lord is my strength and my defense;
> He has become my salvation.
> He is my God, and I will praise Him,
> my father's God, and I will exalt Him.
>
> EXODUS 15:2

Have you ever read about the Israelites and their doubt in God's provision even after they witnessed miracle after miracle? From being freed from slavery to the Red Sea parting for them. From more fresh manna (food) than they could ask for to water rushing from a stone to satisfy their thirst. How could these people be so faithless, you ask? Well, before we start getting too outraged by the Israelites, maybe we should take a good look in the mirror. Have you witnessed miracles? And if so, is there something you are complaining about? Upset about? Sad about? Struggling with that you aren't fully trusting God for?

Think through your life and the ways the Lord has provided for you. I can recall so many moments that now make me wonder why I ever feared. We don't like not having control, but sometimes God permits a setback to happen. He allowed the Israelites trials so He could be their champion at every turn, and He used everything for His glory. "But I will gain glory for Myself through Pharaoh and all his army,

and the Egyptians will know that I am the LORD" (Exodus 14:4). So what do we do? When fear starts creeping up our necks and taking over our thoughts, give it a healthy "Not today, Satan," and then think about the Israelites—the ones we can empathize with in their fear and their worship. These fellow grumblers were watched over, protected, and provided for, and our God is the same today as He was then. Our great Victor will never let you lose.

REFLECT

Think of how God fought for you recently and in the past. In which ways are you currently trusting He is your strength and defense?

God, thank You for fighting my battles. By Your grace, I have seen You move in my life. You've also provided for me even in ways I'm unaware of. Help this heart cease to grumble and complain. You are my Victor, and with You, there is nothing to fear! Amen.

NO SHAME IN HOPE

Now hope does not disappoint,
because the love of God has been poured out
in our hearts by the Holy Spirit
who was given to us.

ROMANS 5:5 NKJV

In two days, my husband will have surgery to remove a tumor, and then the lab will let us know whether it is benign. I'm not writing this devotional from a place dominated by living open-handed, oh no. I'm writing it from a place of needing to live open-handed. How many times can you open your hands with the challenges that come your way before you start to self-protect and expect the worst?

The answer is, with the Lord, an infinite number of times. In challenging situations, it's natural for thoughts to begin from a place of fear. But they don't have to reside there. You may not be experiencing a health scare. The scare could be career-oriented, dating, or a financial hurdle. Whatever uncertainty it is, fear wants to take residence in your situation. And let me tell you, fear is not a cute tenant. It's messy and dark, and it warps reality. So what do you do? While the first natural thought might be fearful, you can help the second one combat it by remembering who's actually in control. The Lord, who sees past, present, and future at once, is in control. The Lord, who works every situation together

for your ultimate good and His glory, is in control. And the Lord loves us so much. Whether this situation results in an inconvenience of surgery or a significant challenge like cancer, I can always keep my hands open and anticipate with hope. And so can you because Scripture is clear. Hope does NOT disappoint. Hope does NOT put us to shame. The immeasurable "love of God has been poured out into our hearts by the Holy Spirit who was given to us" (Romans 5:5), so our hope in God has the same limitations—none. You are in the best hands, so open yours.

REFLECT

Living in hope will not be easy. The enemy wants you to crave control, follow in fear, and pursue pessimism. But remember, hope does not put us to shame. Say that as many times throughout the day as you need to.

Dear Lord, thank You for the supernatural hope we have in You. Help me remember there is nothing to fear because You are in control, and hope does not disappoint. Amen.

CAN'T ALWAYS CONNECT THE DOTS

When Job prayed for his friends,
the Lord restored his fortunes.
In fact, the Lord gave him twice as much as before!

JOB 42:10 NLT

Sometimes, God, in His grace, allows us to look back and connect the dots as to why those challenging circumstances happened. Sometimes, we won't be privy to that reason. The truth remains: God doesn't do anything without a reason. But what if you're stuck in a rut of ruminating and rationalizing? Rather than fixating on the "why," shift your focus to "how." How can I get through this? Well, friend, you know the answer to that. The Lord will never let you go through a challenge without Him.

Think about Job. He is described as "blameless–a man of complete integrity" (Job 1:1). Before Job knew it, his entire world crumbled. His children died, he lost all his money, his body was in severe pain, and his closest friends all asked him to repent of his supposed sin. He explained his innocence countless times and didn't sin against the Lord even when everyone was sure He had! But God didn't give Job a reason as to why Job was going through those trials. Instead, He rebuked him and asked why Job questioned him (Job 40:2)? Job then repented of his ignorance and comprehended that while it rationally didn't make sense because, at the time, people believed that a man's trials were an indication of sin, God would do what God would do, and He was perfect. The Lord blessed Job's faithfulness and restored life to Him in ways more wondrous than Job could have imagined. Job never knew why God allowed those trials in his life, yet he placed God in the seat of honor He deserves. May we all learn to be like Job in that way!

REFLECT

Where are you fixated on finding the reason for a challenge in your life? Where do you need to open your hands and say, "God, You are mighty and mysterious? I trust You even if I can't see one step ahead."

Dear Lord, thank You for watching over us, walking with us, and blessing us. I pray that even if I don't see the reason for a trial, I will trust that You see me and are with me. Amen.

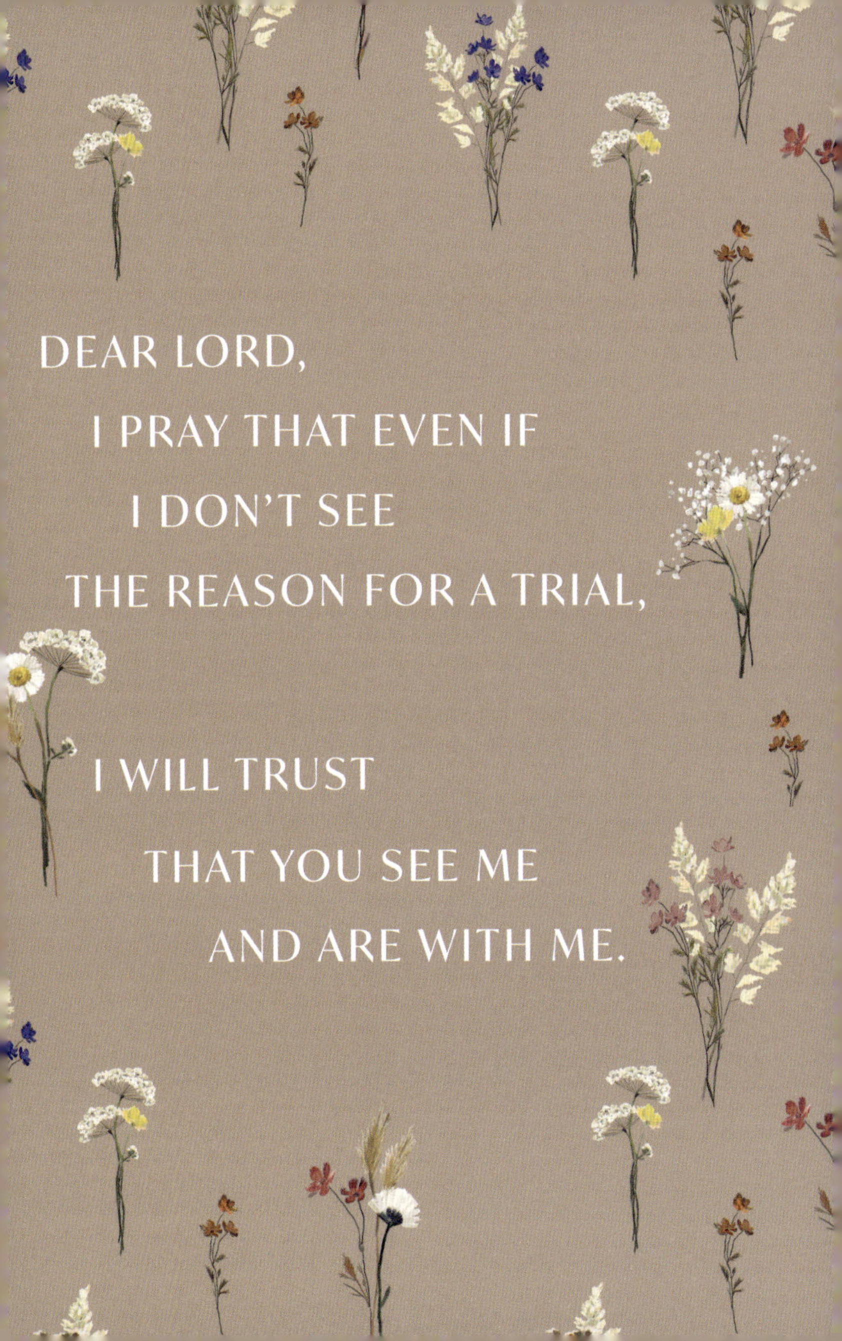
DEAR LORD,
I PRAY THAT EVEN IF
I DON'T SEE
THE REASON FOR A TRIAL,
I WILL TRUST
THAT YOU SEE ME
AND ARE WITH ME.

IT'S PRAISE O'CLOCK

My heart, O God, is steadfast,
my heart is steadfast;
I will sing and make music.
Awake, my soul!

PSALM 57:7–8

When do you find yourself praising God? Is it before a meal? After a prayer is answered? People usually find themselves in states of praise after a high point, such as a celebration or a success. Praising the Lord might feel unnatural during your most significant pain points, but exercising praise in the more challenging times is just as important. Yes, praise is not meant just for times when we are celebrating or thanking God. Learning to encourage our hearts to praise even in the depths of fear and worry is an exercise, and David shows us this well.

In Psalm 57, David writes that he stirs up his heart to sing songs of praise, but he doesn't start there. Saul and his enemies are chasing him. They want the death of David and his downfall. David is hiding, cowering in a cave, desperate and desolate. He prays and asks God to protect him and fight on his behalf. He expresses his fears and every bit he's worried about. Once he has voiced everything weighing him down, he says, "My heart is steadfast; I will sing and make

music. Awake, my soul!" He knows God is faithful and loving and will never let him go. He trusts that God will be glorified across the earth, and even though he is running for his life, he works himself to the point of praise. There is so much we can learn from David, especially when it comes to praising in the hardships. You might not naturally start there, but the truth of God and the hope in God will lead you there.

REFLECT

Have you praised God today? What is keeping you from it? Take the time to voice everything weighing you down so you can come to a point and say, "My heart is steadfast; I will sing and make music. Awake, my soul!"

Dear God in heaven, nothing I am going through right now can keep me from praising You. You are in control of everything, and great is Your love. No matter the distress I feel, I will praise You. In You, I take refuge! Amen.

SURRENDER THE FIGHT

The Lord will fight for you;
you need only to be still.
EXODUS 14:14

One thing about life that we can be sure about is that we are either in a storm or will soon be walking into one. Hurt and aches are, unfortunately, part of human existence. But thanks to faith in Christ, God offers us hope and a future. But what about the present? What about if someone has caused you pain? Be still. God is fighting for you even now. No one can advocate for you more than the Host of heaven. His ears are not closed, and His eyes aren't passing over you. He cares about the pain you feel, and He hears your prayers. He longs for forgiveness to flow from your presence like butter on warm toast. We don't need to let anger consume us because we've been wronged or can't see the path onward.

Think about when the Israelites found themselves trapped between the Red Sea and the mighty Egyptian army. With the vast waters in front of them coupled with the approaching threat of their former oppressors behind them, the uncertainty of their fate had to evoke intense

fear, desperation, and anxiety. It was probably an all-out panic. But when Moses reminded them to keep their eyes on the Lord, who could—and would—deliver them, he said "The Lord will fight for you; you need only to be still" (Exodus 14:14). The same applies to you today! Nothing goes unseen with God. Believe this! He is fighting for you and will deliver you from whatever you face.

REFLECT

Are you stuck in a challenging situation or two? Is there one that is gnawing at your peace? Bring it to God today. Trust that He hears you.

Lord, I trust You with what is weighing on me. You are the One who goes before me and already knows how this works out. I know it works out because You do everything for my good and Your glory. Help me have faith. Help my heart believe this today. Amen.

UNEXPECTED TRANSFORMATION

Do not conform to the pattern of this world,
but be transformed by the renewing of your mind.
Then you will be able to test and approve
what God's will is—His good, pleasing and perfect will.

ROMANS 12:2

"This one is on sale!" I clicked Add to Cart. A pop-up showed another suggested outfit for me. "This is cute too," I said, adding it to the cart. After half an hour, I closed the browser and shut my laptop. Did I buy anything? No. I was indulging in some good old-fashioned consumeristic escapism. I only realized how often I did this once my husband pointed it out. The truth is that escapism can come in several forms, most of which are revered in today's world.

- It could be putting work above everything—so ambitious!
- It could mean consuming through shopping—oh, another sale, I *need* that outfit!
- It could mean never staying put—look at those globetrotters!
- Or it could mean hours spent scrolling, gaming, or sitting in front of a screen—I'm just getting some "me" time, of course!

We get so many mixed messages in today's world. We're told to do whatever makes us happy. We're told that chasing after pleasures, possessions, and power will make us happy. We're told we deserve to escape away from the realities of life. But God didn't make your life so that you need to escape it. He has a good, pleasing, and perfect will, and that also means for your day-to-day! Believe that. When feelings of restlessness or filling a void arise, that is a "pop-up" of your soul craving more time with your Creator. Pick up your Bible, pray often, and listen to what He says. That is the way you renew your mind. And in that transformation, you learn to "test and approve what God's will is—His good, pleasing and perfect will" for your life.

REFLECT

Where are you conforming to the pattern of this world? Dig deep and be honest about this.

Dear Jesus, You didn't create me to chase after possessions or positions. I've been there before and don't want to go there again. True transformation and renewal only come from You. Please help me focus on You and Your good, pleasing, and perfect will. Amen.

THREE PLACES TO LOOK

If then you have been raised with Christ,
seek the things that are above, where Christ is,
seated at the right hand of God.

COLOSSIANS 3:1 ESV

Have you ever wondered why you keep struggling with the same issue? Even when you've done everything right to try to correct it? It's like constantly praying for patience, only to find ourselves faced with situations that test it, and more often than not, stumbling. Then comes the swirly un-fun slide of guilt and shame, but each day brings a fresh start, trusting that God will provide the strength needed for today. Can you relate?

How do we combat what we are tempted by and struggling with? Thankfully, Paul lays it out for God's chosen people in today's Scripture. "Seek the things that are above, where Christ is, seated at the right hand of God." What does this mean?

- Look upward. Jesus, our mighty hope, is seated at the right hand of God. He will never leave you to fend for yourself. What you might have struggled with alone in your "old self" is not something you have to manage and handle alone, with your "new self," meaning who you are in Christ.

- Look outward. God doesn't think in bursts of the short term like we tend to. His plans are for the eternal. You can feel tempted by certain trains of thought and behavior in the short term, but you must change your short-term views to eternal ones.
- Look inward. When you're tempted to indulge in a behavior that you know doesn't align with what God wants for you (Colossians 3:12), train your mind to think about how Jesus has already delivered you from death in eternity, and there is nothing He can't do. The Holy Spirit will not run out on you. Just ask. Jesus has all you need.

REFLECT

Remember who is in control. Where do you need to open your hands and seek the things that are above?

Dear Jesus, help me release any thought patterns that aren't pleasing to You. As one who delights in being raised with Christ, help me seek the things that are above by giving me the power through Your Holy Spirit. Amen.

KEEP YOUR EYES UP

Not only so, but we also glory in our sufferings, because we know that suffering produces perseverance; perseverance, character; and character, hope.

ROMANS 5:3–4

Her eyes look good. I'll see you back in six months," the doctor said. "Wait, what? Really?" I asked in disbelief. With a smile, she said, "Yes, it looks like whatever issues we saw last time aren't currently present." I must have looked perplexed, because the doctor laughed and started explaining further, but I heard nothing more. After several difficult situations, I guess I had come to expect tricky news at this appointment too. I don't know when it happened, but my hopeful heart had shifted to the wary lane. I snapped out of my daze enough to say, "Well, thank You, Jesus!" and call my husband with the good news, but the question lingered in the back of my mind, "When did I stop being hopeful?"

Has it ever felt like the hills keep coming and you barely have time to catch your breath before running up the next one? Hear this: It is okay to feel tired. It is not wrong to feel fatigued. But when you feel like the suffering is too much, like life is out to get you, like you cannot catch a breath, know that this situation isn't meaningless. Even if the doc-

tor had said my daughter had some new complexity, my posture of negativity walking in did not trust the Lord with my future. Because of our hope in Jesus Christ, we can have hope in any trial that comes our way because none of those challenges are pointless. Romans 5:3–4 is clear, "suffering produces perseverance; perseverance, character; and character, hope."

With hope and the confidence God will deliver what He promised, you can continue running the race set before you because, friend, the hard times on this earth won't cease. But thank the Lord, His everlasting hope, which doesn't put us to shame (Romans 5:5), won't either.

REFLECT

Think about a time when suffering produced perseverance in you. Praise the Lord for that. Where do you need to remember your trial isn't pointless? That this too shall pass?

Dear Lord, thank You for the unique ways you allow me to grow in perseverance, character, and hope. Help me rejoice and press on through the fatigue and aches of life, trusting all of it is being used for my good. Amen.

GOD IS IN THE DETAILS

"But seek first His kingdom and His righteousness, and all these things will be given to you as well."

MATTHEW 6:33

Details can encourage your soul more than you know. When did you last pause and notice the details orchestrated by our good God? I am seeing the pieces come together for my husband's surgery tomorrow. Months ago, he took off the day of the surgery and the following day because we were initially going to New York for my work on those days. My toddlers are at my parents' house for a fun week we planned weeks ago. The house we are renting is coincidentally closer to the hospital since our home is on the market. Three significant provisions—time off, childcare, and proximity to the hospital—have already been planned, and none originally were for the surgery.

Cue the tears. Even in the storm, God gives us what we need to weather it with Him, which is our God's nature. He is good, He is omniscient, and His ways are mysterious! All I've done these last four days in waiting is overthink and then surrender my fears to our righteous God. Nobody said seeking first the kingdom of God wasn't messy! When I had last-minute anxiety about planning out the week, I noticed it had already been done. When I see His provision in the details like this, my joy flourishes, and my trust multiplies! And is this not precisely what Jesus encourages us with in Matthew 6:31–32? When we focus on Him, the Lord takes care of the everyday essentials of our lives plus the complex too. "Seek first His kingdom and His righteousness, and all these things will be given to you as well" (Matthew 6:33). Our good Father is walking this road with you, and He will never let you move through life alone.

REFLECT

Consider the situation taking the most energy in your life. Have you noticed the details? Have you taken the time to see how God is very much in them? Do that today. Let your faith be strengthened and encouraged. Let your trust flow.

Dear Lord, thank You for the millions of ways You've been in the details of my life. It is a grace that encourages my faith when I notice them. Please help me focus on Your kingdom and righteousness. Amen.

DAILY MAKEOVERS

Being confident of this,
that He who began a good work in you
will carry it on to completion
until the day of Christ Jesus.

PHILIPPIANS 1:6

Can you remember a time when you were truly frightened? What finally calmed you down? Was it the knowledge that God is always with you? If we truly understand the power of God, then shouldn't we be fearless? We don't burn sage to remove bad vibes, believe specific times or days are more auspicious than others, and use crystals to produce particular results. We know God is invested in us so we can joyfully endure hard moments, months, and even years because they all contribute to our process–being made to be more like Christ.

Every day, we have an opportunity to be made more like Christ. Praise the Lord! We should welcome it! Except, it's not usually comfortable. It might even be what some want crystals and sage for–to prevent hardships and "bad luck." But we know everything works together for our good and God's glory. He's working in us every day. Oh, the freedom that comes with that knowledge. We don't have

to go through life fearful or running from challenges because we know how it will all end—beautiful, holy, and free before our good God. So, however hard it is, welcome the process. How great is our God to make us more like His Son.

REFLECT

How has God made you more like Jesus in the last month? Where do you believe He is working in you today?

Thank You, Lord, for the work You've begun in me and the work You continue to do to make me more like Your perfect and holy Son, Jesus! You will complete this work one day, and I yearn and look forward to that day! Amen.

THE MUNDANE MATTERS

The Lord will work out His plans for my life—
for Your faithful love, O Lord, endures forever.
Don't abandon me, for You made me.

PSALM 138:8 NLT

What an absolute delight it is to know that you are right where you should be. Your waking up today was part of God's plan—the work He has set before you isn't frivolous. Yes, even the mundane. Not one day you've lived was pointless. Yes, even that ordeal. Look at your endurance. Feel the shaping of your character. Behold the hope you have. Your yesterdays were filled to the brim with purpose, and so are your tomorrows. And on top of that promise of purpose, you are not alone. Your Creator is with you.

Does that not flood you with relief? And bring you to praise? Yes, that is exciting, but what exactly is that purpose, you ask? It is uncomplicated, yet we make it so complex! Know the One who made you and love Him. You are His handiwork (Ephesians 2:10), and by spending time with Him, meditating on His Word, and asking the Holy Spirit, you can confidently take the next step in your life with the good work He has begun in you (Philippians 1:6). I know you want to see the following ten steps ahead of you, but rarely is that how the Lord works with us. Each step is a practice of opening our hands and surrendering to His perfect plan for our lives no matter how long it takes, because His love endures forever! He knows everything and every beating heart in this world. What could we possibly know better than Him? He will work out His plans for your life.

REFLECT

What tries to define purpose in your life? Where do you need help to trust the Lord with His plans?

Thank You, Lord, for the perfect plans You have set before me. I pray that You will give me the endurance, patience, and hope to continue doing the work You have begun in me. Thank You, Lord, that You will never, ever let me go. Amen.

OPEN YOUR HANDS

I cry out to God Most High,
to God who fulfills his purpose for me.

PSALM 57:2 ESV

What's one of your biggest fears? Mine is having another child. Well, you might say, then don't. That would be too simple. You see, we want another child. But we do not want a repeat of my third pregnancy, which was filled with weekly appointments, a hematoma, a threatened miscarriage the entire time, preterm labor, the NICU, and so on. But how do I overcome this extreme fear of pregnancy and step forward in faith?

- I don't know that there will be complications. Yet, I am giving my anxiety and fears far more space than they deserve. "Sufficient for the day is its own trouble" (Matthew 6:34 ESV).
- If I believe that God truly works all things together for my good, then even if there were some complications in this additional pregnancy, I would know they weren't without purpose (Romans 8:28).
- I am not promised a child. Nowhere in Scripture does God make that promise. But like a child who comes to his father, I can come to my heavenly Father and ask.

He has the best plans for me, so whether He allows that to happen or keeps that door shut, I can trust He's doing it in love (Matthew 7:7).

- No matter what happens, I will never be alone in it. The Creator of me and the Creator of my potential next child is with me. I could not find more comfort than that (Deuteronomy 31:6).

The truth is, there are what feels like hundreds of verses that I can apply to counsel myself. The Bible holds everything we need to open our hands and trust our mighty, perfect God. Oh, friend, I don't know what you are keeping close to you today, but I hope you will join me in opening your hands to God's purpose for you today.

REFLECT

Living open-handed is a practice; you and I will never fully master it. But we can surrender daily to grow in abundant faith and rich relationship with our loving, powerful God. Where do you need to open your hands?

I cry out to You, God Most High. I open my hands to Your perfect plans. Amen.

THE SPIRIT EMPOWERS YOU

For God has not given us a spirit of fear,
but of power and of love and of a sound mind.

II TIMOTHY 1:7 NKJV

Did you know the average person has forty-five thoughts per minute? I'm not surprised by this because I feel like my mind is a battlefield right now. My husband is currently in surgery for the tumor they discovered last week. My thoughts constantly cycle from fear to surrender to peace. And if I have to do this forty-five times per minute, no wonder I feel tired in the five minutes since he went to the operating room! But really, no one ever said surrender would be an easy process. Whenever an anxious thought plagues our minds, we can dwell in the anxiety or turn away to dwell in God's promises. But we have so many thoughts, and turning away can feel tiring. The good news is, "God has not given us a spirit of fear, but of power and of love and of a sound mind." (II Timothy 1:7 NKJV). So fear does not get the final say, and you don't have to depend on your power. Surrendering fear is a continuous process, and receiving God's peace is too.

Even now, I cycle through my thoughts. Will my husband be okay in surgery? I have no control over what happens in surgery, but the Lord does, and He knows the best plans for my husband. Will the tumor be benign? Again, I have no control over whether it is, but the Lord does, and He has the best plans for my husband. In stressful or challenging situations, the Spirit does not produce fear in God's people. Instead, the Spirit empowers us in our faith, whether that's through courage, patience, peace, or self-control. Ask the Lord to empower you through the Holy Spirit today in the unique ways you need. He's waiting for you.

REFLECT

Where does it seem like fear or anxiety are dwelling in your mind? Cycle through the truth you need so that it helps carry away the anxiety like a cloud passing in the sky.

Dear Lord, thank You so much for the Spirit You've empowered me with. Help me remember You have not given me a Spirit of fear but one of power, love, and of a sound mind. Help me cycle through this truth as many times as I need to. Amen.

FOR GOD
HAS NOT GIVEN US
A SPIRIT OF FEAR,
BUT OF POWER
AND OF LOVE
AND OF A SOUND MIND.
II TIMOTHY 1:7 NKJV

ASK AND ASK SOME MORE

"Ask and it will be given to you;
seek and you will find;
knock and the door will be opened to you."

MATTHEW 7:7

Tell me what is wrong!" I plead with my three-year-old. He huffs and says, "Go away" before stomping away from me for the twentieth time. Although tempting to just let him stomp off, I go to him, pick him up, and hold him, asking again, "What is wrong?" He finally whispers, "You didn't give me milk after dinner." Did the boy ask me for milk after dinner? No, he did not. Did he go from zero to sixty in his wailing? Yes, he did. I sat him down and explained that Mom can't read his mind, and it helps me when he asks me. He surprised me with what he said next. "What if you say no?" I explained that while Mom might say no to what he asks for sometimes, I always want what's best for him, so ask!

Three-year-olds, man. If they aren't a direct reflection of all people and our relationships with God. Matthew 7:7 is so interesting because we've read this a hundred times before, but it wasn't until recently that I read about how some scholars explain that there is a rapidly growing intensity throughout the verse. With each additional verb, the vigor of the asking grows, encouraging the believer not to stop asking. Ask, seek, knock consistently. God is a gracious good Father who has good things for His children. He is listening, and He wants to bless you! How often do we assume the answer is no? Sometimes it will be no, sometimes it will be not yet, but God will always give us an answer. Take the time to ask.

REFLECT

Where have you not asked God because you think you already know His answer? Are you persistent with asking?

Father God, you are El Roi, the God who sees. Even though I forget, help me remember that I can always come to You to ask, just as a child comes to their father. I trust that You will answer my prayers in the way You believe is best. Thank You for listening to me, loving me, and providing for me. Amen.

WHO IS GOD?

She gave this name to the Lord who spoke to her:
"You are the God who sees me," for she said,
"I have now seen the One who sees me."

GENESIS 16:13

Who is this God we should open our hands to and trust with our every day? There are many Aramaic and Hebrew words used in the Bible to represent God. Here are a few:

- He is Abba, which means Father. Think of the ideal father, who has no sin, all love, and perfect plans.
- He is Adonai, meaning Lord Master. Everything belongs to Him, and nothing moves without His knowledge.
- He is El Chay, which means Living God. His works and miracles aren't in the past; they are very much present, and He is with you now.
- He is El Roi, meaning the God who sees.
- He is Jehovah-Rapha, meaning the Lord our Healer. God can heal instantly, through medicine or in eternity. But He always heals.
- He is Elohim, meaning the Creator. God knows you better than you know yourself.

- He is Jehovah-Rohi, meaning the Lord our Shepherd. Our Good Shepherd cares deeply for us, guides us intentionally, and watches over us closely.
- He is Immanuel, meaning God with us. Our Lord is not far away in heaven or sitting on a mountaintop. We do not have to produce, sacrifice, or travel to be with Him.
- He is Jehovah-Jireh, meaning the Lord our Provider. God is a gracious provider and will continue to provide for those who love Him.
- He is Jesus, which means the Lord saves. With Jesus, we have nothing to fear. When life may feel out of control and out of our hands, it is always in the power of the One who saves! The best hands.

REFLECT

Which name of God resonates with you most today? Meditate on that name throughout your day and remind yourself of His promises.

Lord, there are only ten names on this page, but you have countless more! I thank You that You are the God who loves me, saved me from the penalty of sin, and fills me with true joy. Help me remember these assurances! Amen.

CONFESSION BRINGS FREEDOM

If we confess our sins,
he is faithful and just to forgive us our sins and
to cleanse us from all unrighteousness.

I JOHN 1:9 ESV

Living open-handed doesn't mean with just the challenges that come our way or with what is unseen. It also means with what we hold close to our chest, hoping no one else will see. Yes, I am talking about sin—actions or attitudes that are contrary to the will of God. The greatest way to live open-handed when you sin is through confession. Sometimes, we don't want to confess because we think God already knows. He does, but He wants to hear from you. Sometimes, we don't confess because we believe the Lord will punish us. But that is why Jesus paid the penalty of sin. The Lord is faithful and just to forgive us our sins. He cleanses us from all unrighteousness.

So why keep hiding and minimizing your sin? Why not talk to your Savior right now? Why not make it a common practice? One of my most common prayers is, "Lord, search my heart and bring to the surface what I need to confess." He always does because our holiness is of utmost importance

to the Lord! God wants us to experience the peace that comes from knowing we are forgiven and accepted. God longs for us to draw closer to Him, to keep the communication lines open, and to release any shame or guilt that is holding us back from living fully with and for Him.

REFLECT

Do you exercise confession every day when you're with the Lord? Confession brings freedom from sin, closure from the past, and nearness to the Lord. God wants that for you today!

Lord, "if we say we have no sin, we deceive ourselves, and the truth is not in us" (I John 1:8 ESV). Please search my heart today and help me see where I've sinned. Help me make confession a practice in my life so that with the power of the Holy Spirit, I can repent and be made to look more like Jesus! Amen.

JOY IN WAITING

"If you, then, though you are evil,
know how to give good gifts to your children,
how much more will your Father in heaven
give good gifts to those who ask Him!"

MATTHEW 7:11

Waiting is hard! All I can think about right now is whether they will accept our offer. Let me rewind a bit. Thursday night, a notification popped up on my husband's phone for a new listing in one of our favorite neighborhoods we are looking to buy in. Over the weekend, we showed up at the open house and sent in our offer. Now, we are waiting. After more than six months of living in transition, will this finally be where we can be settled for some time?

What are you waiting for right now? Is it a relationship, job, or home? Maybe it's rest, stability, or healing? Whatever it is, there are three truths to remember here. First, God hears you. If you are His, He indeed hears you (Proverbs 15:29). You don't need to provide an offering, pray at a specific time, or say particular words. God hears every prayer that you say any time of day (Psalm 55:16–17). Second, sometimes God will say no or not yet. That doesn't mean He doesn't want good things for you. He might say no because

He loves you and knows the greater plan. If your prayer harms you or hinders you from knowing Him, of course, our good Father is going to say no. His thoughts and ways are higher than we can imagine (Isaiah 55:9). Third, don't stop asking. Pray with hope, ask as a child does with a parent, and trust that one way or another, He will give you precisely what you need. He loves you and wants to provide you with good gifts (Matthew 7:7–11).

Pray with boldness, and wait with peace. There is nothing that God cannot do.

REFLECT

What does waiting look like in your life? This is an excellent measure of how your faith comes into play when pushed to live open-handed. Are you surrendering and finding peace, or are you anxious and ruminating? Dig deep.

Dear Lord, knowing You hear our prayers because we have been reconciled with You by faith in Jesus Christ is a balm to my impatient soul. Please help me find harmony in the waiting today. Amen.

ASK WITHOUT WAVERING

Every good and perfect gift is from above,
coming down from the Father of the heavenly lights,
who does not change like shifting shadows.

JAMES 1:17

I don't think we are in any position to ask God what we want," my friend said. She continued, "God is greater than us. Who are we to ask and think we know better than He does?" I understand where she's coming from. God is perfect, mighty, just, all-knowing, and all-powerful. He certainly knows much more than we do. But Scripture is ripe with encouragement to ask, seek, and knock. Think about James 1. We are told that if we need any wisdom, we ask with complete confidence from the Lord (James 1:5). That is followed by the way we should ask. We don't approach the throne of grace with timidity or doubt (James 1:6). That is comparable to waves of the sea, blown and tossed by the wind! James 1:8 even goes as far as to say that a doubtful asker is "double-minded and unstable in all they do."

We are to approach the throne of grace with confidence, boldness, and trust. The Lord's plan will ultimately come about, and if we trust the Lord, then that is what we want anyway! We want His will to flow through our days and nights, not our own! We can't foresee the domino effect of decisions, but He can. So when He says no to an ask, we trust it is for our betterment, and we can praise Him even in our initial disappointment. When He says yes to our ask, we rejoice, knowing our will and His ultimate will were aligned with that yes. God wants to give His children good and perfect gifts. Approach His throne confidently because of who you are in Christ, ask boldly, do not let doubt take up any space in your belief, and surrender your plans!

REFLECT

The image of waves of the sea, blown and tossed by the wind, is vivid. Where are you not believing God wants to give His children good gifts?

Father of the heavenly lights, I know that every good and perfect gift is from above. While You do not change like shifting shadows, sometimes I do. Help me stay consistent in confidently asking You and trusting Your plans as they roll out. Amen.

THE MOST TRUSTWORTHY FRIEND

Remember the former things, those of long ago;
I am God, and there is no other;
I am God, and there is none like Me.
I make known the end from the beginning,
from ancient times, what is still to come.
I say: "My purpose will stand,
and I will do all that I please."

Isaiah 46:9–10

Where are you in your story? What major, life-impacting decisions and questions are leaving you to feel dizzy in the enigma of it all? Does it have to do with your career or relationship status? Are you trying to decide where to live? Whether or not you should have children? Or maybe you're making decisions for an aging parent? Whatever your big question is, you can trust that God knows how it is going to turn out. He knows what your next steps look like and what your life will entail. Take comfort in know that your loving God is in control. He doesn't have any questions. And His purpose will stand in your life no matter what!

In those moments when you do feel discouraged, "remember the former things." Remember His promise to save His people and how He sent Jesus for us to be reconciled with the Father. There is none like our God. Trust in His goodness. If a friend never failed you, would you trust them? Of course, you would! Rejoice today that God is our most faithful friend. There is none like Him. Open your hands to His purpose today!

REFLECT

If a friend never failed you, would you trust them? Of course. How amazing it is to consider that God is our most faithful friend. What keeps you from trusting that God has it all under control?

All-powerful God, we know that Your purpose will stand, and You will do all You please. In all the chapters of my life, I trust You will care for me in Your mighty, perfect ways. Amen.

THE PIMPLES OF LIFE

A person's wisdom yields patience;
it is to one's glory to overlook an offense.

PROVERBS 19:11

Did you know there are people who are make a living out of popping pimples and posting about it online? What a time we live in! Sometimes, pimples leave scars, spread, or grow back more belligerently when you mess with them. But they can be so annoying, painful, and front-and-center that it makes sense why some prefer to pop them. However, taking an approach of overlooking the "pimples of life" blesses us. Instead of diving head-on with hefty words or trying to find an immediate solution for the offenses and insults hurled our way, it helps to overlook an offense. It helps to forgive. It helps to have grace like the grace we receive daily.

Is it uncomfortable? Yes. Sometimes, does it feel like it's right in the epicenter of your face? Absolutely. Would you get more satisfaction from bursting it even if it meant that it could get messy? Sure. But all of that is a form of wanting to control the situation. We can never control someone else's actions toward us. We aren't God. We don't know everything

that is going on behind the scenes, and we most certainly aren't the ones administering justice. So lean into patience. Ask the Holy Spirit today to flood you with patience for the one who has offended you. God will make everything right in His time, and you and I don't have to squeeze a thing.

REFLECT

Where are you holding an offense close to your chest? Have you tried to work through forgiving? Forgiveness does not mean friendship, but it does mean faith in God's timing, plans, and justice.

Dear Lord, age doesn't bring about patience, but wisdom does. Please give me more opportunities to exercise patience and grow me in wisdom through Your Holy Spirit. Amen.

NO PLACE SAFER

I will both lie down in peace, and sleep;
For You alone, O Lord,
make me dwell in safety.

PSALM 4:8 NKJV

We've lived through some wild times—recessions, pandemics, and natural disasters, to name a few. When you learn more about everything happening around you and pair that with everything happening in your day-to-day life, it's natural to be overwhelmed.

You know who else had a lot going on? Our boy David. Yes, King David. David's enemies were vast in number, and their power and influence increased daily. Worst of all, people were telling David to give up because God had abandoned him and to accept his destruction.

But David knew that with the Lord, he had nothing to fear. He could have paced and kept a lookout night and day, but he went directly to the Lord, surrendered his problems, and asked Him to fight for him. David also knew that true safety comes from being with the Lord. Think back to a time when you experienced a sense of security, relaxation, and contentment, like being wrapped in a warm blanket of assurance. This is the way the Lord watches over us night

and day. So that fear that is creeping within you, eating away at your peace? Bring it to Him today. God is waiting to give you the true peace only He can!

REFLECT

Even in complete chaos, the Lord's peace prevails. Where do you need to believe that God is your refuge? Talk to Him about that today.

Lord, You promise to be with us no matter what happens around us (Isaiah 41:10). You control everything, from every sparrow in the air to every hair on our heads (Matthew 10:29–31). You offer us peace in the storm (Psalm 46:1–3). Help me trust you like David! Help me lie down and sleep tonight in complete peace, no matter what is happening around me. Amen.

92%

"Therefore I tell you, do not worry about your life,
what you will eat or drink; or about your body,
what you will wear. Is not life more than food,
and the body more than clothes? . . .
Can any one of you by worrying
add a single hour to your life?"

MATTHEW 6:25, 27

Science has shown us time and time again that worrying can lead to an increase in chronic conditions and a shorter lifespan. Scripture repeatedly tells us not to worry and that you cannot add a single hour to your life by worrying. So why do we still worry? The anticipation of an unfavorable future event causes worry. And according to researchers at Penn State University, only about 8 percent of the things people worry about come true. That means 92 percent of what you're worried about will not happen. Can you imagine how much time you'd get back, how much peace you'd protect, and how much joy you'd maintain if you didn't allow your worries to take up as much space as they covet?

It's true—life hurls curveballs sometimes, and your brain wants to visualize every probable outcome. We are waiting on the results of my husband's tumor, so believe me, I get this. When we called at the forty-eight-hour mark, they

told us the results would be shared at the seven-day mark instead. My first reaction was, "Are you kidding me?" However, after time with the Lord, I decided to stop focusing on the outcomes because sitting on pins and needles ruins reality, and God has much planned for today if I get out of my head to see it. He's never given us a reason not to trust Him, and we must remember that truth in our impatience and worry! Even in unfavorable circumstances, remember that God uses every situation for His purpose. We have nothing to lose.

REFLECT

Jesus tells us clearly that there is nothing to gain by being worried or anxious. Yet we continue to worry. Today, surrender your worries to the Lord and receive His peace. Instill this practice in your life every day.

Dear Lord, help me transform the time I spend on worrying into time that honors You. Please help me, with the power of the Holy Spirit, trust You in all things at all times. Amen.

TEARS IN A BOTTLE

"I have heard your prayer,
I have seen your tears;
surely I will heal you."
II KINGS 20:5 NKJV

When was the last time you cried? Maybe it was today. Or maybe it was yesterday when Google Photos reminded you of an easier time, of what life was like years ago, and the soppy tears just started falling. Are tears in negative situations a lack of faith in the Lord? No. God sees our tears, and He hears our prayers. Not only that, but with the intricate way He's made our bodies, there are also many benefits to crying, such as healthy coping and a significant release of oxytocin and endorphins. God knows every tiny tear that has escaped your eyes and the weight of what they hold. "You keep track of all my sorrows. You have collected all my tears in your bottle" (Psalm 56:8 NLT).

In II Kings 20:5, God tells Isaiah that He has heard Hezekiah's prayer and will heal him. Does that mean God will heal me when I cry, pray, and ask Him to? This is where it gets tricky. The healing in this passage is specific to Hezekiah, as not everyone who prays for healing receives it in this life. But everyone in this life has their prayers heard

and their tears seen by God. The way healing happens is entirely in the Lord's hands, but come what may, He will restore you in this life or after. So keep praying. Keep crying out. Keep asking for healing. This truth is what encourages me on the days when my fears snarl in my ear. There is no such thing as too many tears, prayers, and requests for the Lord from His people.

REFLECT

The Lord is your good Father, who wants to see you in a posture of surrender and trusting Him with everything on your mind. Where do you need to release, whether through crying, praying, or trusting? Maybe all three?

Dear Lord, You see my tears. It brings me so much comfort to know that You see me even in my sorrows, where words escape me and salty tears dribble down my cheeks. Help me surrender whatever brings me to tears, and help me trust You with it all! Amen.

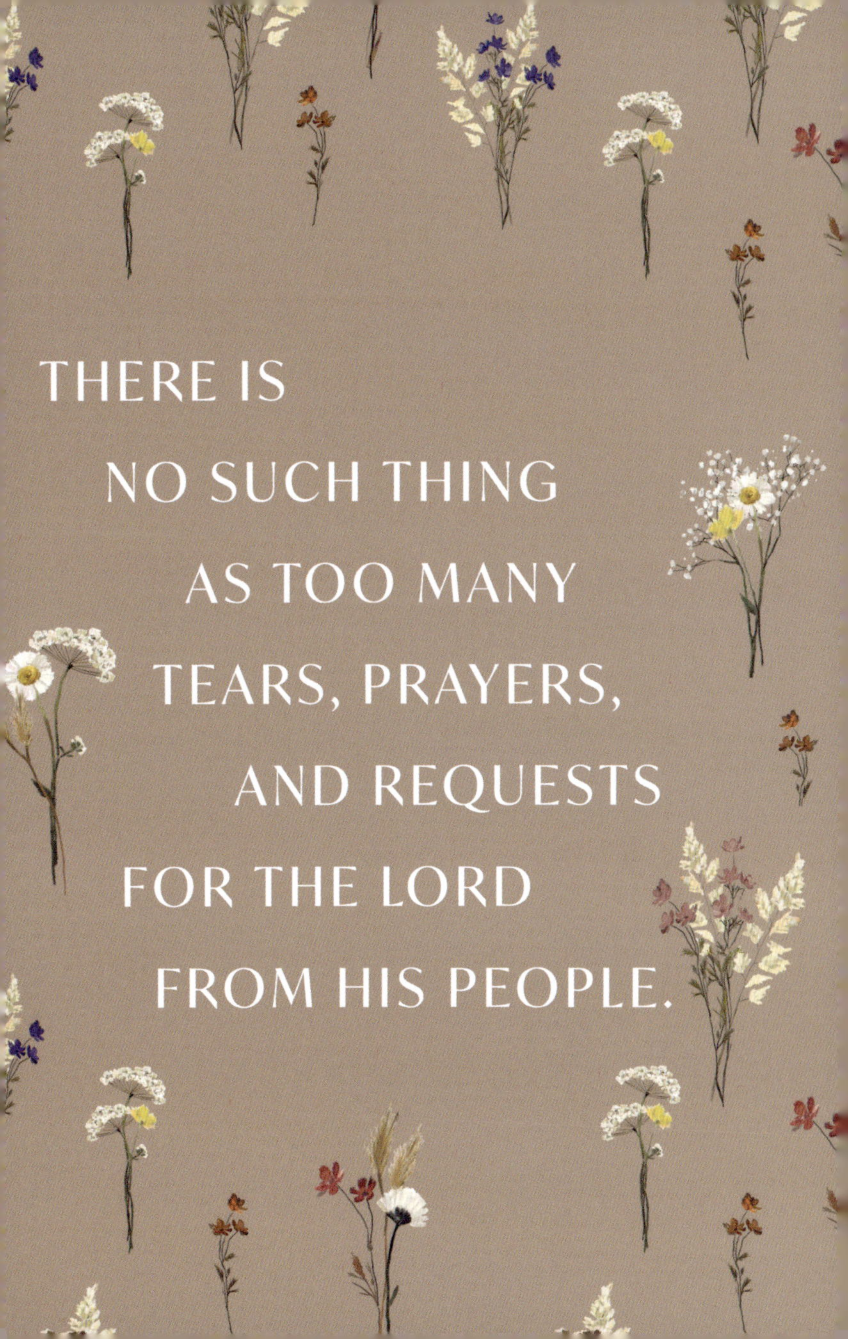
THERE IS
NO SUCH THING
AS TOO MANY
TEARS, PRAYERS,
AND REQUESTS
FOR THE LORD
FROM HIS PEOPLE.

IT'S TWO ACTIONS, NOT ONE

He must increase,
but I must decrease.
JOHN 3:30 ESV

Let me take you behind the scenes as a professional Instagrammer. It's nothing to grind away for five to nine organic or paid posts a week. The good thing about social media is that it has the potential to be a place for sharing the gospel, encouragement, and prayer. Social media can also be a feeding ground for your idols, meaning something you give more of yourself to than God. You can feed your power idol with more followers. You can feed your vanity with more likes. You can feed your insecurity with validation. You can feed your anger with rage-baited information. You can feed just about anything with social media. It's a battlefield, and anyone who enters this space needs to have a healthy relationship with discipline, accountability, and repentance. The sad truth is that social media isn't the only place like this. Our world places so much value on grabbing power, influence, and prestige. But Scripture encourages us in the complete opposite direction.

John the Baptist says it best, "He must increase, but I must decrease." When you read that, what do you think?

Make Jesus greater in your life? Yes, but that's only half of it. Two actions are happening. We must actively try not to make ourselves great. The more we decrease, the more God has the space and place in our lives to increase. John the Baptist's followers may not have wanted to believe that John wasn't equal to Jesus, but John tried to make it as clear as he could several times. Even if John was tempted by their worship, he never let that sway him. He knew he had no business having that level of power, influence, and might to construct his own kingdom. And neither do we. The more he decreased, the more Jesus increased in his life and the world.

REFLECT

Where are you building your own kingdom? Where are you holding back from giving it all to God?

God, You don't want part of our lives. You want all of us. You are better than anything we can run after. Help me actively decrease any greatness I seek so that You increase. Amen.

WANT HIS WILL ABOVE ALL ELSE

This is the confidence
we have in approaching God:
that if we ask anything
according to His will, He hears us.

I JOHN 5:14

What is it that you want with all your heart at this very moment? Did you know that God wants to give you the desires of your heart? That He wants to give you everything that He knows is good for you in the long run? Ask God today that if it is His will, to make a way for your hopes to come true. Ask Him to release you from any feelings of anticipation to self-protect, and know that you can live in excited expectation of all that God has for you.

And then when you find yourself, possibly months or years later, sitting in victory, you will feel the sweetness of God's love for you. So undeserved.

But for now, don't doubt good things, even when you face challenges. Try hard not to dread, doubt, or disengage in an attempt to self-protect, but confidently approach God with both hands. Throw yourself toward love, hope, and surrender fully. Ask God for His will to be done, and know

that when you are aligned with Him, you are in the safest place. Your eternity is secure because of faith in Christ. And in this chaotic, sporadic life, that is an extraordinary foundation.

REFLECT

What do we have to fear here? Ask your good Father, be confident, and pray for your will to align with your Father's!

Dear Lord, if my desires don't align with Your will, take those desires away from me. I want to live in Your will because it's the best place I can be! Amen.

JOY IS OUR PORTION

"Do not let your heart be troubled;
believe in God, believe also in Me.
In My Father's house are many rooms;
if that were not so, I would have told you,
because I am going there to prepare a place for you.
And if I go and prepare a place for you,
I am coming again and will take you to Myself,
so that where I am, there you also will be."

JOHN 14:1–3 NASB

The tumor is cancerous," my husband said. I was on the phone with him at a different hospital, waiting for my daughter's MRI to finish. My head swirled with a million thoughts. *What does this mean for him? For our family? For our future?* My heart was troubled, and I didn't know what to read or pray, so I looked up Scripture for a troubled heart. Sometimes, it really is as simple as that. "Do not let your hearts be troubled; believe in God, believe also in Me" (John 14:1). In this Scripture, Jesus talks to His disciples after sharing that many trials are coming their way; even one of His disciples will betray Him. They are understandably in a panic, and He encourages them not to be troubled but to take heart and trust in God and Him. He is honest with them

about the tumultuous path ahead and shows them the way through it. He ends His reassurance by sharing His promises of restoration. Not only will we eventually be where He is, but Jesus Himself will take us there. That is an unbelievable promise that should make us rejoice! Remembering who was in control of this tumor and our next steps, and even life after this, eased my troubled heart significantly. No matter what happens, the end is already accounted for, and it is so good.

REFLECT

Where is your heart troubled? Surrender that to God today. Believe He is with you, loves you, and has the best plans for you, because He does!

Dear Lord, You knew when you would be betrayed by one of Your own, and You continued faithfully so that we may experience restoration with the Father. Help me walk faithfully, trusting in Your greater plan and surrendering anything that troubles my heart. Joy is my portion and available today even now. Amen.

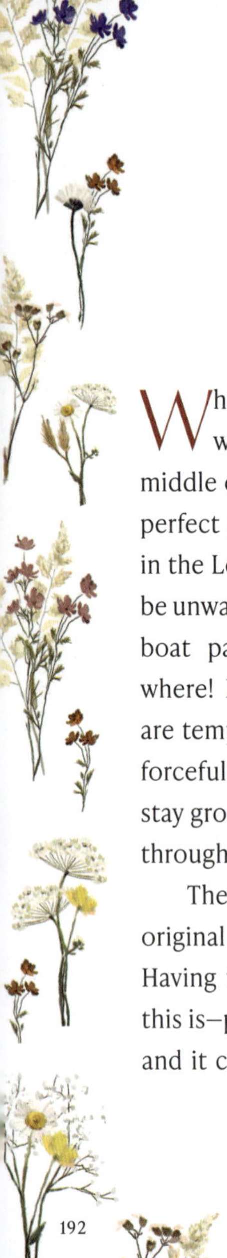

SHALOM AND EIRENE

You will keep him in perfect peace
whose mind is stayed on You.

ISAIAH 26:3 NKJV

When was the last time you had perfect peace? Was it when everything was going well? What about in the middle of heavy challenges? Scripture tells us we can have perfect peace at any time as long as our mind is anchored in the Lord. Have you seen a boat's anchor before? It must be unwaveringly reliable, or else you'll have some miserable boat passengers accidentally traveling to who knows where! Boat anchors also are not a permanent fix. They are temporary and must be readjusted because waves can forcefully hit the boat. Our minds are the same way. We will stay grounded when we can anchor our minds on the Lord through repeated prayer, surrender, and praise.

The Hebrew word for peace is *shalom*, and in the original text, perfect peace is expressed as *shalom shalom*. Having this word repeated emphasizes the kind of peace this is—perfect. The Greek word for perfect peace is *eirene*, and it comes from the verb *eiro*, which means "to weave, to join together." Weaving our thoughts and emotions with the Lord results in perfect peace, regardless of circumstances. There is peace with God that nothing in this world can take away from you! To be in perfect peace means to be complete or whole and to keep our minds on Him. No lost sailor at sea here!

REFLECT

Check in with yourself. Are you experiencing God's perfect peace today? What is keeping you from being steadfast and anchoring your mind in Him?

Dear Lord, thank You for Your perfect peace. Nothing in this world can take it away from me. My circumstances do not define the peace You have ready for me. Help me stay steadfast and keep my mind on You. Amen.

IT'S THAT SIMPLE

Rejoice always, pray without ceasing,
in everything give thanks.
I THESSALONIANS 5:16–18 NKJV

One thing about rejoicing always is that it will look weird to people who don't believe in Jesus. People can think you're overly optimistic, toxic positive, or in denial of reality. But the hope we have in Jesus isn't hanging by a string. It's not on the petals of a dandelion flying away. It's not based on the alignment of the planets or some pretty rocks from the ground. Our hope is a confident expectation in Jesus Christ. We know He's come before, and He will come again. And there is so much to rejoice in that hope!

After receiving my daughter's Down syndrome diagnosis, my husband and I prayed for peace and joy. We felt those prayers answered within a week of that initial diagnosis call. Our peace wasn't based on feeling confident in our parenting ability, and our joy wasn't from a sudden head full of knowledge about her diagnosis. They came without any understanding, which can only be from above! With time, we've had increased peace and joy with our daughter's diagnosis as we've delved into her world and met more people in the same community. We are so grateful for that. But in the beginning, it was only by God's grace and mighty hand that we had peace and joy beyond understanding.

There is not one thing you can think about, or that weighs on you, that you cannot bring to the feet of God. He says to rejoice in hope, so let your hope be known! He says to be patient in tribulation, so slow down when trying to problem solve it all! He says to be constant in prayer. Do not just start with prayer, but be constant (Romans 12:12). I'll choose this confident, carefully curated path by the Creator over one of crystals, cards, and chance any day.

REFLECT

Paul encourages us that regular thanksgiving should be a distinctive mark in a Christian's life. Be realistic: Do you find yourself rejoicing more than you worry or fear? Trials don't have the power to hinder your thankfulness.

Dear God, Your will is so clear for me. You want me to rejoice, pray, and give thanks. Why do I make it more complicated? Please help me by the power of Your Holy Spirit to live in your will for me today. Amen.

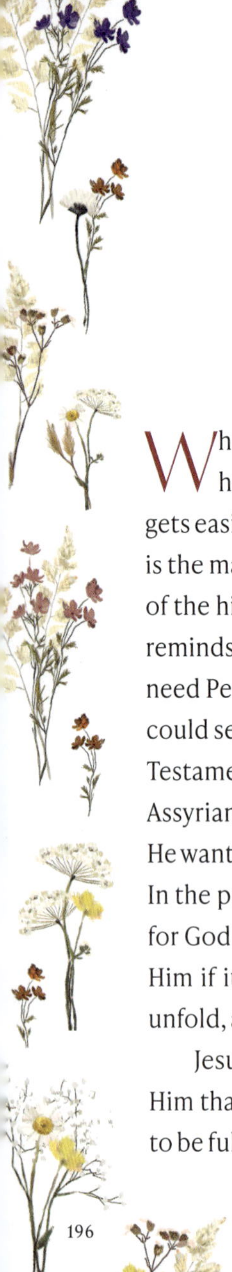

TRUST HIM IN THE NO

"Do you think I cannot call on My Father, and He will at once put at My disposal more than twelve legions of angels?"

MATTHEW 26:53

When the answer is no after you've asked and asked, how do you move forward? Judas's betrayal never gets easier to read. When Judas kisses Jesus to signal that this is the man to arrest, Peter, in his rage, cuts off the ear of one of the high priests who have come to arrest Jesus. But Jesus reminds Peter that this is part of God's plan. Jesus doesn't need Peter to defend Him; He has His Father in heaven, who could send 72,000 angels to protect Him if asked. In the Old Testament, a single angel is credited with killing 185,000 Assyrian soldiers (II Kings 19:35), so He has a killer defense if He wants it. And yet, Jesus knows this is what the Father wills. In the previous verses, we see that Jesus prayed three times for God to take the cup, or the impending cross, away from Him if it was God's will. However, the events continued to unfold, and Jesus, seeking to do the Father's will, continued.

Jesus could have asked for legions of angels to defend Him that night, but He did not. He knew the Scriptures had to be fulfilled. Oh, friend, I hope you find this as encouraging as I do! Even when this life brings us pain and hardship we can't believe, and we know it will, we stand secure because we know we are fulfilling God's purposes for us and where we are going after this. Nothing is wasted with God! He can use everything for our good and His glory; look no further than the cross. These circumstances in life will never have the final say. Imagine it with me—perfect peace, no pain, and only eternal joy. Thank You, Jesus.

REFLECT

God tells us to ask often (Matthew 7:7), but sometimes, He says no. In those moments, do you submit to His will or hold fast to your own plans like Peter with his sword?

Dear God, help me align my will with Yours. Even in the challenging times when I cannot see two steps ahead of me, help me trust You. I know You are with me always. Amen.

SURRENDER THE RESULTS

Rejoice in our confident hope.
Be patient in trouble,
and keep on praying.

ROMANS 12:12 NLT

Oh, it's her doctor with her MRI results!" I exclaimed at my husband. Let me rewind a second. We were waiting for my daughter's MRI results to see if she was eligible for hearing implants. When we had learned she had profound hearing loss and was legally deaf six weeks earlier, we were shocked and, transparently, heartbroken. But we accepted the diagnosis and trusted that God had a good plan for her life. We went to Romans 12, which talks about how to live according to the incredible mercy God has given us, and remembered to "rejoice in our confident hope, be patient in trouble, and keep on praying"! And pray we did. We prayed constantly that the Lord would give her the option for implants if it was His will for her life, and in the meantime, we started learning ASL. And now, her doctor was calling with the results.

The doctor was very guarded when he let us know that she had no nerve in her left ear, so she would not be able to get an implant there. I closed my eyes as he moved to her

right ear. That pause felt like days. He let us know that she had the nerve she'd need for an implant in her right ear and to make an appointment for the next steps. We rejoiced!! I'm sure the doctor thought he was sharing okay news with us, but having been seated in the unknown for months and learning our daughter could get this implant made my heart explode with joy! It's all about perspective. When we are bent down, relying on God to get us through each day and give us His joy and peace, we rejoice often! We don't take life's victories or blessings for granted. Challenges and trials help us remember where our hope and strength come from and how God will never let us navigate life alone. Even if this were not the outcome, God would still be good. He never changes, and that is always a reason to rejoice. Thank You, Jesus, for Your undeserved blessings.

REFLECT

Romans 12:12 is short but mighty with actions. What situations in your own life come to mind?

Dear Lord, thank You for
Your incredible mercy, and please help me
live according to that gift. Amen.

HIS REFUGE IS JOY

But let all who take refuge in You
rejoice let them sing joyful praises forever.
Spread Your protection over them,
that all who love Your name may be filled with joy.

PSALM 5:11 NLT

Are you ever stunned with how much time young kids want to spend with their parents? Children want to feel secure and comfortable and to know they are loved and cared for—and parents give this sense of belonging to them like no one else can. God wants that with all of His children too. He wants you to trust Him, believe in Him, and enjoy Him. We have nothing to fear or want when we are with our Father. He gives us everything we need and is our source of joy (Psalm 43:4). Do you believe that? Do you live in that truth? In Psalm 5:11, David shares a prayer, asking for all who entrust their lives to God be able to rejoice!

So often, when our cups are full, we have an overflow of joy for the people around us. Was this the case with David and why he wanted everyone around him to rejoice too? Just two verses before, we saw that David was asking for vengeance and holy judgment for his enemies (Psalm 5:9–10) and facing a significant trial himself (II Samuel 15:13–14), so no! David wasn't joyful because of his circumstances. David was joyful because his life was in the Lord's hands, and he trusted Him. God alone lifts our heads when difficult circumstances surround us. No matter what is going on in your life at this very moment, you can take refuge in our perfect Father today and rejoice. Open your hands to it, friend!

REFLECT

The Lord is holy, gracious, merciful, and faithful to His promises. Where are you disbelieving that today?

Dear Lord, thank You that my circumstances do not dictate my joy. Please help me remember that even in the wildest of waves, You are my staunch source of joy. Amen.

SCRAP THE SARAPPIM

When anxiety was great within me,
your consolation brought me joy.

PSALM 94:19

Have you ever had too much caffeine? It is not a feeling I wish on anyone. I remember googling "ways to reduce caffeine jitters," and one recommended source said to eat eggs with garlic, so I ate two eggs covered in garlic and then lay on the ground until the jitters disappeared. It should come as no surprise that I didn't eat eggs for an extended time after that. It's okay to laugh at me; I deserve it! That feeling of physical unease coursing through my body from the caffeine was overwhelming! And there are still times I wish I could cook up a couple of eggs when my mind follows suit. We need a living and active consolation for soul-level jitters, not eggs and garlic. Thankfully, God's Word is just that (Hebrews 4:12).

When your thoughts are vast and vexing, a surefire way to calm your soul is to remember God's consolations. Does God understand why I'm anxious? Our God is not a God who is foreign to suffering, but instead, we have a sympathetic high priest in Jesus who experienced every temptation and vast sorrow (Hebrews 4:15). Will God leave me alone? He will

walk with you in every single journey you are on. Nothing will separate you from His love (Romans 8:37–39). Does God hear me? Yes! Always. Every prayer (Psalm 116:2). How He answers is up to His perfect will. And there are so many more consolations I could share! When the multitude of your thoughts feels overwhelming, exhale with relief that our God is all-knowing, all-powerful, all-present, and all-loving, and His promises never fail.

REFLECT

The original Hebrew for anxious thoughts is sarappim. *These "disquieted thoughts" are described as uneasy, restless, and on edge. Where are those thoughts pervasive in your life today? What promises of God do you need to remind yourself of?*

Perfect God, thank You so much for Your vast promises covering me in protection and peace. Please help me remember to set my mind on You. Help me turn from my disquieted thoughts and embrace Your perfect promises for my every day today. Amen.

UNEXPECTED TEACHERS

Rejoice in the Lord always.
Again I will say, rejoice!

PHILIPPIANS 4:4 NKJV

It was one of those mornings when my kids woke me up before the sun. I grumbled out of bed and started the day an hour or two before I was ready. My patience was low, and my mood was lower. In the car, my daughter started talking about how thankful she was that God made trees. And then I heard my son respond to her by saying, "I am so grateful He made the birds." They went back and forth like that for a couple of minutes, saying everything they were thankful for that God did, and I just wanted to cry. Kids can be such excellent teachers with their unfiltered spirits.

Philippians 4:4 says, "Rejoice in the Lord always. Again I will say, rejoice!" When I'm tired or walking through a difficult season, that command feels not just hard but impossible. But my kids reminded me with their genuine thanks of the necessity of pausing and rejoicing in the Lord. Praising our perfect God and all He has done for us, from the cross to being our constant companion, fills you up in ways sleep or coffee cannot. When we focus on fellowship with Christ and the blessings around us, we enjoy God and experience peace through His power. Sometimes we adults overthink rejoicing. We think we need ideal circumstances to rejoice. Scripture is clear. We can rejoice always. God is always good, so why wouldn't we rejoice in Him often? I joined my kids that morning. Thank You, God, for the roads; thank You, God, for the birds; thank You, God, for the trees. Thank You, God, for my kids and for how they point me back to You.

REFLECT:

With the spirit of a child, can you unabashedly list all the reasons you rejoice today? Say it out loud!

God, You are so gracious for it all! In every circumstance, I can rejoice. I can rejoice even when the wind feels strong and the storms pour down. Help me see that throughout my day today. Amen.

WE CAN
REJOICE ALWAYS.
GOD IS
ALWAYS GOOD,
SO WHY WOULDN'T
WE REJOICE
IN HIM OFTEN?

Dear Friend,

This book was prayerfully crafted with you, the reader, in mind. Every word, every sentence, every page was thoughtfully written, designed, and packaged to encourage you—right where you are this very moment. At DaySpring, our vision is to see every person experience the life-changing message of God's love. So, as we worked through rough drafts, design changes, edits, and details, we prayed for you to deeply experience His unfailing love, indescribable peace, and pure joy. It is our sincere hope that through these Truth-filled pages your heart will be blessed, knowing that God cares about you—your desires and disappointments, your challenges and dreams.

He knows. He cares. He loves you unconditionally.

BLESSINGS!
THE DAYSPRING BOOK TEAM